# The End of Order

D1722205

**Francis Fukuyama** is Professor of Public Policy and director of
the Center for Global Political Economy at
George Mason University in Virginia.
He was formerly a senior researcher at the Rand Corporation and
policy advisor at the State Department in Washington DC.

In 1989 he published an article entitled 'The End of History' in
*The National Interest* journal. This article, which
provoked enormous controversy was subsequently developed into
the world-wide best selling book, *The End of History*.
His book, *Trust*, on the sources and constraints on social capital was
published to great acclaim in 1995.
He is currently working on *The Great Disruption* to be published in 1999.

# The End of Order

FRANCIS FUKUYAMA

The Social Market Foundation
September 1997

First published by The Social Market Foundation, 1997
in association with Profile Books Ltd

The Social Market Foundation
11 Tufton Street
London SW1P 3QB

Profile Books Ltd
62 Queen Anne Street
London W1M 9LA

Tanner Lectures on Human Values, University of Utah Press, Vol. 18, 1997

Printed in Great Britain by Biddles Ltd

A CIP catalogue record for this book is available from the British Library.

Paper No. 3

ISBN 1 874097 860

# Contents

# Figures and Tables

# Foreword

It is now eight years since Francis Fukuyama announced the 'end of history', which to him meant the end of ideology. Bill Clinton's re-election followed by Tony Blair's election landslide have led both men to say that we are presiding over post-ideological politics, where the limits of debate are set by arguments about effectiveness in public policy. In this new world, 'what counts is what works'.

In one sense, Fukuyama takes comfort from the fact that both Britain and the United States are now being governed from the 'radical centre'. For him it is proof positive of how narrow the realm of political, ideological and economic choice has become. Everyone accepts that we are being integrated into the global economy and that we must play by its rules. But as Fukuyama demonstrated in the Tanner Foundation lectures delivered at Brasenose College, Oxford, and published in full here, how societies cope with the consequences of that integration is the subject of intense political, some would say ideological, debate. There may be substantially less disagreement about the role of governments in economic life than there was a decade ago, but questions about whether there has been a decline in social cohesion, what has been responsible for it and if there is anything that can done are the subject of fierce disagreement. Fukuyama's own contribution to that debate in *The End of Order* is to say that the undermining of the family and marriage is central to social breakdown. The primary engine for generating the social capital which societies need to function properly is increasingly under strain.

This may be an unremarkable observation. However his explanation for it is more contentious. A combination of oral contraception and greater female participation in the labour market has led to what he calls 'the Great Disruption', a period of social upheaval not seen since the industrial revolution. The *raison d'être* for marriage has collapsed. Men no longer feel constrained to limit their fertility to the women and children they can support economically. Women can no longer rely on men and are increasingly supporting themselves and their offspring independently or through the state instead. The result is that an entire generation is growing up without fathers to socialize them, a generation which is more prone to educational failure, violence and criminality than its predecessors.

How then to address these problems? Fukuyama says that turning back the clock is undesirable and in any case impossible. New ways must be found of producing the social capital which is the buttress against social breakdown. Governments have their part to play, particularly in addressing the problem of employability among low-skilled males, but just as the state crowded out private capital formation by pursuing inappropriate economic policies in the past, so now it should resist quick fixes in social policy which risk crowding out social capital formation. For some, this will leave the answers to the questions Fukuyama raises uncomfortably open-ended. Others will see a parallel with the last Great Disruption at the time of the Industrial Revolution, which led to the remoralisation of Victorian society by forces other than government. Either way it is clear that the debate is far from over – which means that ideology has not yet been put to bed.

Roderick Nye
September 1997

# Part 1:
# The Great Disruption

Since the fall of the Berlin Wall, there has been an extraordinary amount of attention paid to the interrelated issues of social capital, civil society, trust and social norms as central issues for contemporary democracies. The propensity for civil society was said to be an essential condition for the transition to stable democracy in Eastern Europe, and the decline in social capital in the United States is said to be a major problem for American democracy today. I have argued elsewhere that social capital is an important and relatively under-studied factor in explaining certain characteristics of the global economy.[1]

In contrast to the related concept of human capital, there is less consensus today about what social capital is, how it can be measured, where it comes from and particularly how to get more of it. I want to address each of these issues, and in particular how social capital is produced and consumed in an increasingly complex, high-tech economy like that of the United States.

# Social capital: definitions

The first use of the term 'social capital' that I am aware of was in Jane Jacobs' classic work *The Death and Life of Great American Cities* (1961), in which she explained that the dense social networks in older, mixed-use urban neighbourhoods constituted a form of social capital, and was far more responsible for cleanliness, absence of street crime and other quality-of-life measures than were formal institutional factors like police protection.[2] The economist Glenn Loury, as well as the sociologist Ivan Light, used the term 'social capital' in the 1970s to describe the problem of inner-city economic development: African-Americans lacked the bonds of trust and social connectedness within their own communities that existed for Asian-American and other ethnic groups, which went a long way towards explaining the relative lack of black small business development.[3] In the 1980s, the term was brought into wider use by the sociologist James Coleman and the political scientist Robert Putnam, the latter of whom has stimulated an intense debate over the role of social capital and civil society in both Italy and the United States.[4]

Social capital can be defined simply as the existence of a certain set of informal values or norms shared among members of a group that permit co-operation among them. The sharing of values and norms does not in itself produce social capital, because the values may be the wrong ones. This point can be illustrated simply. Southern Italy is a region of the world that is almost universally characterized as lacking in generalized social capital and trust. This does not mean that there are not strong social norms. Diego Gambetta recounts the following story:

A retired [Mafia] boss recounted that when he was a young boy, his mafioso father made him climb a wall and then invited him to jump, promising to catch him. He at first refused, but his father insisted until finally he jumped – and promptly landed flat on his face. The wisdom his father sought to convey was summed up by these words: 'You must learn to distrust even your parents.[5]

The Mafia is characterized by an extremely strong internal

code of behaviour, *l'omerta*, and individual mafiosi are spoken of as 'men of honour'. Nevertheless, these norms do not apply outside a small circle of mafiosi; for the rest of Sicilian society, the prevailing norms can be described more as 'take advantage of people outside your immediate family at every occasion otherwise they will take advantage of you first'. Obviously, such norms do not promote social co-operation and the negative consequences for both government and economic development have been extensively documented.[6]

The norms that produce social capital, by contrast, must substantively include virtues like truth-telling, the meeting of obligations and reciprocity. Not surprisingly, these norms overlap to a significant degree with the Puritan values Max Weber found critical to the development of Western capitalism.

It is clear that the norms that produce social capital are partible, that is, they can only be shared among limited groups of people, not among others in the same society. While social capital exists in all societies, it can distributed in very different ways. Families are obviously universally important sources. But the family structure differs from one society to another and the strength of family bonds differs, not simply from family ties in other societies, but relative to other types of social tie. In some cases, there appears to be something of an inverse relationship between the bonds of trust and reciprocity within kinship groups and between kin and non-kin; while one is very strong, the other is very weak. What made the Reformation important for Weber was not so much that it encouraged honesty, reciprocity and thrift among individuals, but that these virtues were for the first time widely practised outside the family.[7]

It is perfectly possible to form successful groups in the absence of social capital, using a variety of formal co-ordination mechanisms like contracts, hierarchies, constitutions, legal systems and the like. But informal norms greatly reduce the transaction costs entailed by these mechanisms, and under certain circumstances may facilitate a higher degree of group adaptation. Civil society, which has been the focus of considerable democratic theorizing in recent years, is in large measure the product of social capital, though in certain important respects not completely congruent with it.

There are two points that need to be made about social capital. First of all, it is not a subset of human capital because it is a property of groups and not individuals. Conventional human capital – education and skills – can be acquired by Robinson Crusoe on his proverbial desert island. The norms underlying social capital, by contrast, must be shared by more than one individual to have any meaning. The group endowed with social capital may be as small as two friends who share information or collaborate on a common project or it can be as large as an entire nation.

Second, social capital is not necessarily a good thing, with regard to either politics or economics. Co-ordination is necessary for all social activity, whether good or bad. Socrates, responding to Thrasymachos' contention that justice was merely the advantage of the stronger, notes in Book I of the *Republic* that even a band of robbers must have a sense of justice among themselves, or else they could not succeed in pulling off their robberies. The Mafia and the Ku Klux Klan, for example, are both social groups who are violent and murder but who are nonetheless constituent parts of American civil society. In economic life, group co-ordination is necessary for a form of production, but when technology or markets change, a different type of co-ordination with perhaps a different set of group members becomes necessary. Bonds of social reciprocity that facilitated production in the earlier time period become obstacles to production later. To continue the economic metaphor, social capital at that point can be said to be obsolete and needs to be depreciated in the society's capital accounts.

# Social capital and the broader problem of modernity

The debate over American social capital reflects a much broader and more important question: whether, as economic development progresses, we are witnessing an unravelling of the larger Enlightenment project of building a modern world order based on the rule of reason. The modern liberal project envisioned replacing a community based on tradition, religion, race or culture with one based on a formal social contract among rational individuals who come together to preserve their natural rights as human beings. Rather than seeking the moral improvement of their members, modern societies have sought to create institutions like constitutional government and market-based exchange to regulate individual behaviour.

From the earliest days of the Enlightenment, conservative thinkers like Burke and de Maistre argued that such a community could not work. Without the transcendental sanctions posed by religion, without the irrational attachments, loyalties and duties borne out of culture and historical tradition, modern societies would come apart at the seams.

Other thinkers less hostile to the Enlightenment have nonetheless recognized the importance of moral norms in the functioning of modern liberal democracy. Most important was Tocqueville, who wrote extensively on the kinds of moral habits and customs necessary to sustain a system of limited government. It was Tocqueville, of course, who pointed to the American 'art of association' as underpinning the dense and complex civil society in the United States; an art that served as a school for democratic self-government and permitted the self-organization of large sectors of American society.

It has long been recognized that economic modernization brings in its wake changes in fundamental values and norms; indeed, the entire discipline of sociology has been described as one long commentary on the shift from *Gemeinschaft* to *Gesellschaft*. In the heyday of 'modernization theory' in the 1950s and early 1960s, this value shift – from traditional to modern, from ascriptive to voluntary, from status to achievement – was largely regarded as a difficult but positive and necessary transition societies had to go through before they stabilized around the tidy norms of contemporary suburban America. The problem was that values did not stop evolving and the shift towards a post-industrial society that gathered steam in the 1960s seemed to be accompanied by a new set of norms – particularly the deterioration of the nuclear family and a rise in various forms of social deviance – that were not so obviously healthy.

One consequence is that earlier arguments about the self-undermining character of the Enlightenment have been revived by a number of thinkers in recent years. John Gray, for example, has argued that the social deterioration apparent in contemporary America marks the inevitable disintegration of the Enlightenment experiment.[8] Modern societies based on Enlightenment principles – constitutional democracy in the political sphere and the capitalist market – have succeeded, according to this line of thought, only because they have been able to live off several centuries of accumulated social capital. That is, the social constraints formerly provided by religion and other norm-creating cultural institutions have survived into the current secular age only out of a kind of reflexive habit, but such societies are ultimately unable to generate new social capital.

Fears that the stock of social capital is being depleted are not new, they were around during the late nineteenth century transitions from agrarian to industrial societies in Europe and North America. Social capital had new and unexpected sources in these industrial societies. It is useful to revisit some of the broader questions of macrosociology raised at that time, for at least two reasons. First, since the great classics of sociology describing the earlier transition were written, there has been another massive shift in social norms and, I would argue, decline in older forms of social capital for which some account needs to be given. Second, we now have data on a number of non-Western modernized societies – primarily in Asia – that will serve as useful points of comparison in trying to understand whether these shifts in norms are the product of modernization *per se*, or rather the particular path modernization has taken in the West.

# The problem of measurement

Robert Putnam has argued that the quality of governance in the different regions of Italy is correlated with social capital, and that social capital has been in decline in the United States since the 1960s. I do not want to engage in a prolonged discussion of the so-called Putnam debate in this context, except to use it to illustrate some of the difficulties involved in measuring social capital. Putnam has been very ingenious in coming up with a wide variety of statistical measures of social capital, both in *Making Democracy Work* (1993) and in 'Bowling Alone' (1995).[9] These include information on groups and group membership, such as data from the General Social Survey, survey research on values (such as the World Values Survey) concerning perceptions of honesty and trust and measures of political participation such as voter registration and newspaper readership. Putnam has collected time-series and cross-sectional data on groups from sports clubs and choral societies to trade unions and political parties.

Much of the debate over Putnam's research concerns the empirical validity of his basic finding that American social capital has been declining over the past two generations. Numerous scholars have either pointed to contradictory data showing groups and group membership to have been actually *increasing* over the time period covered by Putnam, or else that the available data simply do not capture the reality of group life in a complex society like that of the United States.[10] By definition, a newly formed group will be less institutionalized than a more established one, and hence less likely to keep good statistical information on itself, or to be observed by third parties collecting statistics on group memberships. There are a large number of informal social networks for which no data exist at all. On the other hand, Putnam excludes from his measures social capital in families, for which abundant evidence of decline exist.

There are three further measurement problems (see Appendix p.125). First, social capital has an important qualitative dimension. While a bowling league or garden club might be, as Tocqueville suggests, schools for co-operation and public-spiritedness, they are obviously very different institutions from the United States Marine Corps or the Mormon Church, in terms of the kinds of collective action they foster. A full account of social capital needs to take account of the degree of cohesive action of which a group is capable.

The second problem has to do with what one might call the positive externalities of group membership. While all groups require some degree of social capital to operate, some build bonds of trust and hence social capital outside of their own memberships. As Weber indicated, Puritanism mandated honesty not simply towards other members of one's religious community, but towards all human beings. On the other hand, norms of reciprocity can be shared among only a small subset of a group's members. While what Putnam terms a 'membership group' like the American Association of Retired People (AARP) has a huge membership, there is no reason to think any two given members will trust one another or achieve co-ordinated action just because they have paid their yearly dues to the same organization.

The final problem concerns negative externalities. Some groups actively promote intolerance, hatred and even violence toward non-members. While the Ku Klux Klan, Nation of Islam and Michigan Militia possess social capital, a society made up of such groups would not be particularly appealing and might even cease to be a democracy. Not only do such groups have problems co-operating with each other, the bonds of community uniting them are likely to make them less adaptive by isolating them from influences in the surrounding environment.

It should be clear that finding a believable number expressing the stock of social capital for a large and complex society like the United States is next to impossible. We have empirical data, of varying reliability, on only a certain subset of the groups that actually exist, and no consensus means of judging their qualitative differences.

There is, however, an alternative method of estimating a nation's stock of social capital that poses fewer measurement problems. Instead of measuring social capital as a positive value, it might be easier to measure the *absence* of social capital through traditional measures of social deviance, such as crime rates, family breakdown, drug use, litigation, suicide, tax evasion and the like. The presumption is that since social capital reflects the existence of co-operative behavioural norms, social deviance *ipso facto* reflects a lack of social capital. Data on social deviance, while hardly unproblematic, is far more abundant than data on social capital and is also available on a comparative basis.

It should be stated at the outset that there is one very serious problem with using social deviance data as a negative measure of social capital: it ignores distribution. Just as conventional capital is unevenly distributed within a society (i.e. as measured by wealth distribution studies), so social capital is also likely to be unevenly distributed: strata of highly-socialized, self-organizing people may coexist with pockets of extreme atomization and social pathology. Using social deviance as a proxy for social capital is similar to using poverty data as a measure of a society's overall wealth, circumstances which would show the United States as one of the poorest countries in the OECD in absolute terms.

Nonetheless, it is still useful to look at comparative social deviance data in and of itself as indicators of trends in social capital. In many Western societies, beginning with the United States, social deviance has been growing at such a rapid rate it can scarcely fail to affect the performance of the society as a whole.

# The Great Disruption

Social norms have been subject to continuous change throughout human history, and for the societies that have experienced industrialization and economic modernization, the rate of change has moved to higher levels since these processes began.

That being said, it is striking how rapidly norms have shifted throughout the industrialized world in the three decades between approximately 1965 and 1995. The rate of change in a variety of social indicators has been so great that this entire period deserves to be characterized as a 'Great Disruption' in earlier patterns of social life.

The primary change that has occurred has been a decline of the nuclear family. As I will argue below, there is substantial evidence that this decline is linked causally to a whole series of changes in social norms or outcomes, including crime, child abuse, poverty, educational achievement and, ultimately, the kind of civic engagement with which Putnam has been concerned. The reasons why this decline occurred are, needless to say, complex, and arise out of the interaction of certain economic and technological changes and social norms and values. In the sections that follow, I will present empirical evidence documenting the Great Disruption and then discuss alternative explanations for why it occurred.

## Breakdown of the nuclear family

In light of the massive evidence that the nuclear family is in long-term decline, it is remarkable how many social scientists continue to assert that no significant change has occurred. The sociologist David Popenoe notes that in the very years the Great Disruption was taking place, it was common for sociology textbooks to heap scorn on the 'myth of family decline'.[11] In the 1950s and early 1960s, this may have reflected the fact that family cohesion in America and Western Europe actually improved, as did fertility rates during the 'baby boom'. After the large but temporary disruptions to social patterns brought on by the Second World War, a number of social indicators – particularly the homicide and divorce rates in the United States – actually improved over their pre-war levels.

In the late 1960s, 1970s and 1980s, however, the indicators began to turn downwards very dramatically and social scientists began using other strategies to reinterpret the data and reassure people nothing sinister was happening. The most common was what Daniel Patrick Moynihan has called 'defining deviancy down': as the incidence of divorce, single-parent families and illegitimate births increased, the definition of the family was stretched to include virtually any type of household, whether or not it included a mother, father and their biological children. In this period the US Census Bureau replaced the term 'illegitimate births' with the more morally neutral phrase 'births to unmarried women'. It was commonly asserted that each generation tended to see the norms of the preceding one nostalgically and failed to see the problem that caused those norms to change in the first place.[12] Many feminists had no love for the patriarchal nuclear family of the 1950s and had strong ideological motives for accepting alternatives to it.

**Divorce**

FIGURE 1.1 shows the American divorce rate from 1920 to 1994. Discounting a war-induced rise in divorces, the rate of change increases very dramatically after about 1967. While it levelled off in the 1980s, this does not so much reflect an increase in marital stability as the passing of the baby boom cohort through the age when they are most likely to divorce. Approximately half of all marriages contracted in the 1980s in America could be expected to end in divorce.

**Figure 1.1: Divorces per 1,000 population, 1920–1994, US**

The ratio of divorced to married persons (FIGURE 1.2) has increased at an even more rapid rate due also to a parallel decline in marriage rates; for the country as a whole this rate has increased over fourfold in the space of just thirty years.[13]

It has been widely recognized that North American social patterns are exceptional and differ substantially from other industrialized countries.[14] The United States has always been significantly more individualistic, had a smaller welfare state and generally exhibited higher levels of social deviance than most European states, particularly those of continental and Northern Europe. Many American observers trace the breakdown of the nuclear family to specifically American cultural factors, such as the youth counterculture and the crisis of authoritative American institutions in the wake of

**Figure 1.2: Ratio of divorced persons per 1,000 married persons, US**

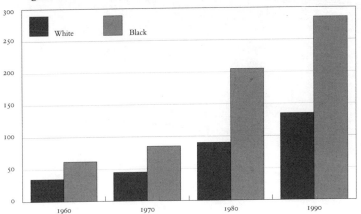

the Vietnam War and Watergate scandals.

FIGURE 1.3 (on the next page) shows that virtually every country in Europe has experienced a massive increase in divorce levels, and in many cases the rate of change has been as high as that of the United States. After settling down from wartime disruption in the 1950s, families began breaking apart in Europe around the same time as in the United States. There are some individual variants – West Germany and France have relatively lower rates while the Nordic countries and the United Kingdom have higher ones. Other European Catholic countries like Italy, Spain and Portugal did not legalize divorce until rather late in this period (1970, 1981 and 1974 respectively); once legal, however, divorce rates began to climb rapidly in those societies as well (see TABLES 1.1 and 1.2).[15]

As FIGURE 1.4 indicates, the United States started and ended with a higher divorce rate than any country in

Figure 1.3: Crude divorce rates, 1950–1991, Europe

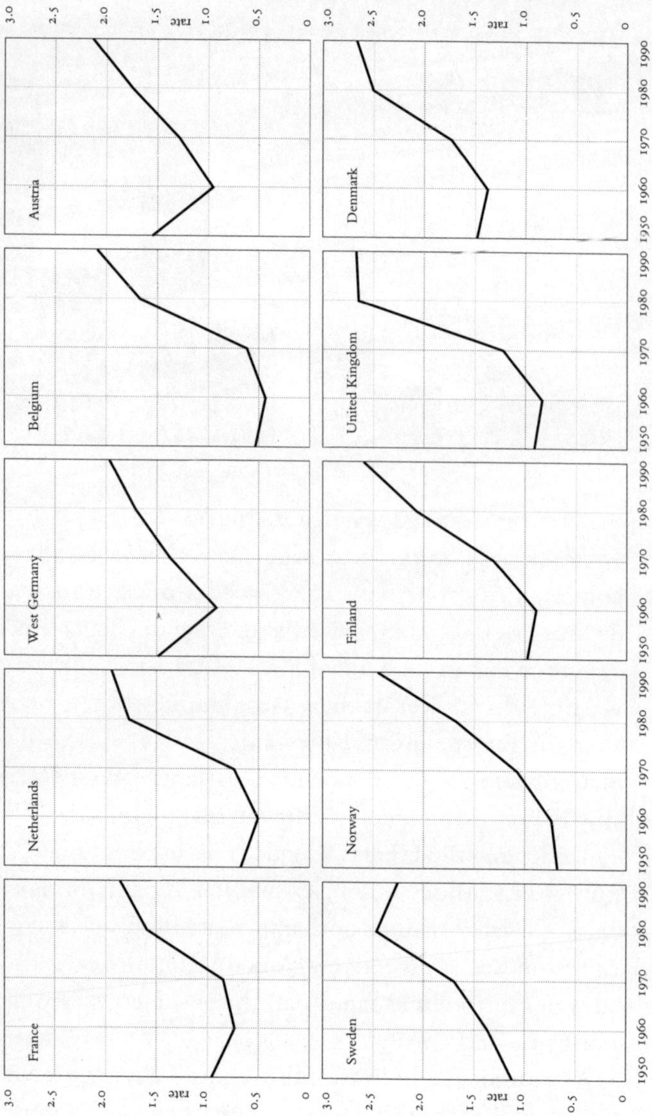

**Figure 1.4: Crude divorce rates, 1950–1990**

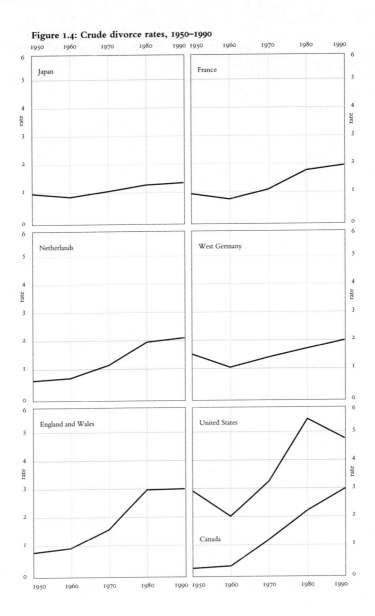

**Table 1.1: Crude rates of Marital Dissolution in Italy per 1,000 population, 1971-1988**

|                  | 1971 | 1975 | 1980 | 1986 | 1988 |
|------------------|------|------|------|------|------|
| legal separation | 0.32 | 0.19 | 0.21 | 0.29 | 0.44 |
| divorce          | 0.32 | 0.6  | 0.21 |      | 0.44 |

Source: William J. Goode, *World Change in Divorce Patterns*, Yale University Press, New Haven, 1993, p. 57.

**Table 1.2: Divorce and separation suits filed in Spain, 1981-1988**

|            | 1,981 | 1,985  | 1,988  |
|------------|-------|--------|--------|
| divorce    | 9,483 | 18,291 | 22,449 |
| separation | 6,880 | 25,046 | 33,240 |

Source: Goode, 1993, p. 71.

Europe. The chart also indicates another outlier within the larger group of OECD countries: Japan, whose rate has increased only modestly over the post-war period.

## Illegitimacy

Higher divorce rates have meant larger numbers of children growing up without both parents at home. In addition, steadily increasing proportions of children have been born out-of-wedlock. In the United States, births to unmarried women as a proportion of live births climbed from under 5 per cent to 31 per cent between 1940 to 1993.[16]

A number of observers have pointed out that the reason why the percentage of out-of-wedlock births has increased so dramatically is less because of an increase in the number of births to unmarried women than as a result of a steep drop in the fertility of married women.[17] This is sometimes

Figure 1.5: Births to unmarried mothers as % of all births by racial category, US

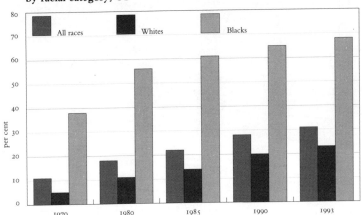

adduced to argue that the relatively high present-day American illegitimacy rate should not be of concern. It is not really clear why the fact that women best able to care for and raise children properly have decided to have fewer, while those less able to do so are having more, should be considered reassuring. Moreover, the increase in fertility of unmarried women is not trivial, having moved from about 12 live births per 1,000 women to about 50 between 1950 and 1990.[18] Furthermore, it is clear that illegitimacy is not spread out evenly among communities in the United States. Rather, it tends to be concentrated in certain particular sectors where fatherlessness has become a virtual norm. FIGURE 1.5 (above) traces the number of births to unmarried women in America from 1970 to 1993 as a percentage of all births. While African-Americans started this period having greater absolute numbers of illegitimate children than whites, whites have caught up rapidly. Fatherlessness is the

**Figure 1.6: Illegitimacy rates, 1960–1990**

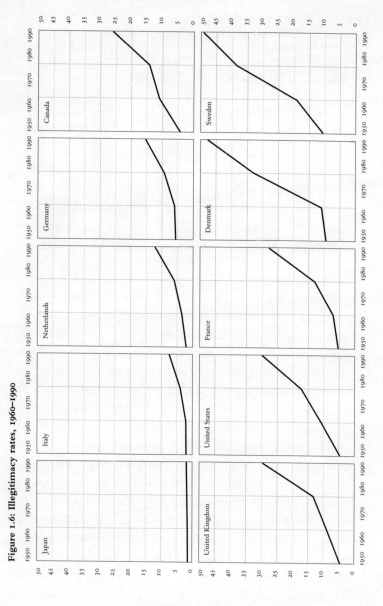

condition of a significant majority of black American children, and in certain areas of concentrated poverty having a father married to one's mother can be an extremely rare occurrence. It is interesting to note, incidentally, that the overall illegitimacy rate for America as a whole is now higher than the rate for the black community in the mid-1960s when Moynihan wrote his famous report on the black family.[19]

If we turn from the United States to the OECD world, we find the United States is no longer such an outlier and that virtually all industrialized countries, again with the exception of Japan, have experienced extremely rapid rises in illegitimacy rates (see FIGURE 1.6 opposite). While some countries like France and the United Kingdom saw increases in their rates somewhat later than America, the increases when they came were even more dramatic. In Scandinavia, illegitimacy rates are the highest in the world and significantly greater than the United States. (The meaning of illegitimacy in Scandinavia and other parts of Europe is different from the United States insofar as unmarried cohabitation is much more common; many 'illegitimate', children grow up in a household with their biological parents.) Again, within Europe, Germany has relatively low rates, while Italy's rates are lower still, reflecting, apparently, the delayed liberalization of divorce laws.

It should be noted that from the standpoint of child welfare, being born to a single mother is only part of a broader social problem. Of children born to married parents in the United States in the 1990s, about 45 per cent will see their parents divorce by the time they are eighteen.[20] In subcommunities like African-Americans, the percentage is much higher, making the experience of continuously living with two biological parents throughout one's childhood relatively unusual. These kinds of rates are not without historical precedent – in colonial America, fewer than half of all children reached the age of eighteen with both of their biological parents still living.[21] The difference, of course, was that in the eighteenth century, the loss was overwhelmingly due to disease and early mortality, while in the late twentieth century it is largely a matter of parental choice.

## Crime

Despite considerable publicity about declining crime rates in the United States during the early 1990s, violent crime has diminished only to the levels of the early 1980s and remains high relative to the entire post-war period. FIGURE 1.7 traces the American homicide rate during the post-war period, while FIGURE 1.8 indicates that the property crime rate has increased in a roughly parallel fashion.

It has long been recognized that American crime rates are significantly higher than in other industrialized countries. This was true before the beginning of the Great Disruption and continues to hold true today. FIGURE 1.9 (on page 26) illustrates the difference in rates for homicide and rape between the United States and selected other industrialized countries

The reasons for the relatively high rates of violent crime in the United States has been the subject of prolonged analysis by criminologists. This is an issue to which I will return. Homicide rates have been going up in other

**Figure 1.7: Homicides, per 1,000 population, 1950–1994, US**

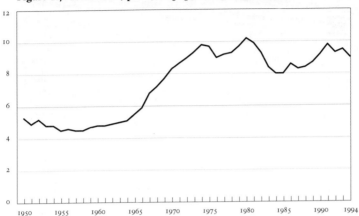

**Figure 1.8: Property crimes, per 100,000 population, US**

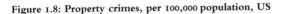

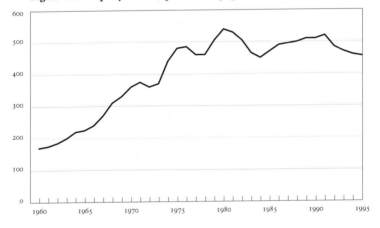

industrialized countries as well, though not at anything like the rates experienced in the United States. We should note, however, that there have been substantial increases in property crime rates throughout the OECD world (again with

**Figure 1.9: Violent crime rates, 1984**

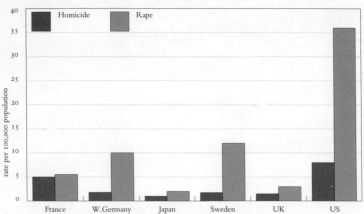

**Figure 1.10: Property crime rates, 1984**

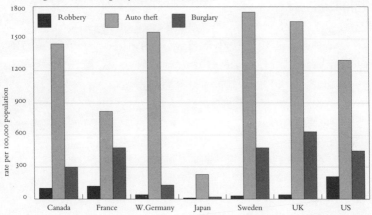

the exception of Japan). FIGURE 1.10 (above) shows the United States is not the leader in several categories of non-violent crime.[22]

**Figure 1.11: Teenage drug use, 1974–1994, US**

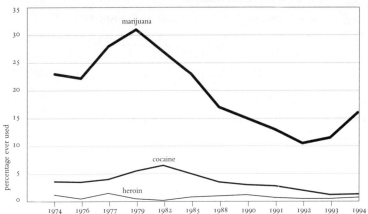

## Child Abuse

There have been a number of well-publicised child abuse *causes célèbres* in America, Belgium and other countries in recent years, and again evidence that rates have been increasing over roughly the same period. There has also been evidence of certain hysteria over the subject, fed by overzealous prosecutors and journalists. Officially reported American abuse cases, including physical and sexual abuse, emotional and physical neglect, have risen steadily through the 1990s according to the US Census Bureau.

## Alcoholism and Drug Abuse

The one area in which there has been substantial improvement in social indicators is drug use. Since peaking in the 1970s, drug use in the United States has gradually decreased, though as Republican challenger Bob Dole made clear in the 1996 presidential campaign, rates of teenage drug use began rising again from 1993 onwards. FIGURE 1.11 shows rates of marijuana, cocaine and heroin use in the United States between 1974 and 1994. The rates for alcohol use have also declined marginally for all age groups over this period.

# Explanations for the 'Great Disruption'

As the preceding statistics indicate, the changes in social norms that I have labelled the Great Disruption have been massive in their cumulative scope, rapid and spread over a very wide range of countries. Large social phenomena of this sort generally have a variety of interrelated causes, and indeed observers have attributed these changes to factors such as poverty and economic disruption, shifts in cultural values, feminism and the movement of women into the labour force, government policy, including levels and types of welfare benefits, changing technology, television and other forms of mass communication, inherent defects in liberal ideology, the decline of religion and the like.

Given this multiple causality, it is impossible to sort out fully which of these factors is the most important, or even to establish the direction of the causality between phenomena that appear to be statistically correlated. One consequence is that various groups are able to emphasize their favoured causal factor and adduce plausible evidence showing that theirs is the primary factory involved. The available evidence will not permit us to establish causal relationships to satisfy all observers, but the data does permit us to evaluate and, in some cases eliminate, certain causal claims as insufficient to explain more than a small part of the phenomenon.

## Social norms and the new science of human nature

Any account of social norms needs to be embedded in a broader theory of norm-generation. In Part 3, I will attempt to present the outlines of such a theory, but it is important to note at the outset that intellectual trends in this area have been undergoing rapid changes under the weight of a growing body of empirical evidence concerning the origins of behavioural norms.

It is safe to say that for the greater part of the twentieth century, most social scientists have believed that social norms – at least the sorts of social norms relevant to the question of social capital – are socially constructed. Clifford Geertz, dean of an older generation of cultural anthropologists, argued that culture began to evolve prior to the completion of the evolution of the human brain. This implied, to him, that there was no clearly demarcated natural substrate that linked different human societies and that cultural rules were therefore entirely relative to the societies that generated them. The 'science' of cultural anthropology, therefore, was not devoted to the discovery of cultural regularities across societies, but rather to the 'thick description' of individual cultures in all of their particularism.[23] B. F. Skinner's school of behavioural psychology maintained that the human brain resembled Locke's *tabula rasa* prior to its reception of environmental stimuli after birth, a view extended even to the acquisition of language.[24] Neo-classical economics, for its part, has a highly developed branch – game theory – devoted to the generation of co-operative social norms by rational actors. The belief in the social construction of norms was particularly strong in discussions of gender-related issues, where feminist scholars tended to assert that observed differences between males and females reflected not differences in genetic endowments, but the cumulative effects of generations of 'patriarchy' and norms established by male domination.

Over the past generation, however, a tremendous amount of research has been carried out in the related fields of evolutionary psychology, socio-biology and evolutionary genetics which cumulatively has had the effect of restoring a concept of human nature as the starting point for any social science.[25] Evolutionary psychologists, for example, start from the view that any given set of genetic endowments in an organism exists by virtue of its adaptive significance at some earlier stage in the organism's evolution. The characteristics subject to genetic influence are not simply physical ones, but mental attributes as well, many of which produce behavioural regularities not simply across human cultures, but across different animal species. Evolutionary psychology has produced a series of testable hypotheses about human behaviour that has received substantial empirical confirmation. While most of these studies have not been able to connect these behavioural regularities to specific parts of the human genome, there is good reason to expect this will occur over the next few decades.[26]

Evolutionary psychologists have uncovered behavioural regularities that have a direct bearing on the question of social capital. Take, for example, the question of altruism.

Richard Dawkins has made us all aware that, contrary to Marx, man is not a 'species being', i.e. does not have a genetic predisposition to sacrifice his individual interests for the sake of the survival of the species as a whole or even for the sake of larger collectivities like nations or tribes.[27] On the other hand, there is substantial evidence that altruism is the rule among individual organisms sharing genes or gene sequences, and indeed that the degree of altruism is strictly proportional to the degree of genetic overlap. Thus parents can be expected to exhibit unreciprocated altruism to their children and to their siblings; they practice a lesser degree of altruism toward cousins and nephews with whom they share half as many genes, but still a greater degree than towards second cousins or complete strangers.

The power of this approach is illustrated in the work of the anthropologists Martin Daly and Margot Wilson on homicide.[28] Daly and Wilson argue that from a neo-Darwinian point of view, the incidence of homicide should be inversely proportional to the genetic relatedness of the murder and the victim. After an exhaustive study of police records, they showed that contrary to the popular perception that most murders take place within families, the rate of homicide is in fact lower among biological relatives as the theory would suggest. That is, given the same opportunities to commit murder, murder of non-genetically related spouses or step-relatives is far more common than the murder of children by parents, brothers by brothers etc.

There is also evidence that the norm of reciprocity – that is, the willingness to return a favour for a favour or a harm for a harm, is not, as game theorists would expect, something that arises through the interactive playing of games by individual agents, but is rather hard-wired into the genetic code not only of human beings but of other animal species as well.[29] While the norm of reciprocity may well have originated historically in a game-theoretic manner and serves the narrow interests of the individual organism, it is practised by each individual not as a result of individual learning in each present time period, nor out of rules inherited through purely cultural mechanisms, but through genetic inheritance.

There may be other social behaviours that are now genetically coded into human behaviour. The anthropologist Lionel Tiger has argued that certain primate males have a propensity to small-group co-operation outside of kinship – so-called 'male bonding' – that has had its origins in the requirements of hunting in the hunter-gatherer societies that shaped present-day human psychology.[30]

# The evolutionary role of the family

Some of the most important findings to come out of the natural sciences in recent years concern the differing psychological backgrounds of men and women, and their implications for gender relations, the family and kinship. Based on the pioneering work of William J. Hamilton on parental investment, evolutionary psychologists have observed that males and females follow very different reproductive strategies. From a neo-Darwinian point of view, the interest of an individual organism is to get its genes passed on into the next (and successive) generations. For females, reproductive strategy involves commanding sufficient economic resources to protect themselves and their offspring until the latter are able to take care of themselves. Males, by contrast, require a far lower level of parental investment to get their genes into the next generation, and their strategy therefore involves spreading their genes as widely as possible.

These differing reproductive requirements lead to different psychological proclivities that correspond to our common-sense perception of the difference between women and men. Females necessarily tend to emphasize the quality of their mates over sheer numbers, since they cannot increase their fertility past a certain natural limit, and because the mate's quality – often measured by economic resources – will be critical to the survival of the mother's offspring. Males, on the other hand, can get their genes into the next generation with a minimum of parental investment, simply by mating with as many females as possible. This difference in strategy accounts for a wide variety of phenomena: that males tend to be more promiscuous than females; that male and female jealousy differs (males will care more if their mates had sex with another partner, since this will imply non-paternity, while females will be more concerned with emotional involvement, since this may mean loss of economic resources)[31]; and that high-status males (and not high-status females) will tend to accumulate multiple partners.

One of the staples of post-war cultural anthropology was the seemingly infinite variety of kinship relations across human cultures, and indeed the changing nature of kinship across time within a single culture like that of Western

Europe. Cultural relativism was born in a climate that saw only difference and particularisms among all of these varying practices.

Contrary to Clifford Geertz, however, there are in fact many cultural universals that appear to be grounded in nature rather than culture.[32] As Lionel Tiger and Robin Fox have pointed out, while kinship practices vary widely between cultures, the evolutionary function of kinship does not.[33] The function of kinship is to reconcile competing male and female reproductive strategies through an exchange of fertility (controlled by the female) for economic resources (almost always controlled by the male). This exchange can take the form of the bourgeois family of Western Europe and the United States in the 1950s, but need not. From the woman's standpoint, the chief objective is protection and resources for herself and her offspring through the reproductive cycle, and it does not matter whether those benefits come from a husband, the husband's male relatives, her brothers or a larger kinship group. The variety of actual kinship relationships thus masks a commonality of function in terms of reproduction.[34]

An understanding of the natural substrate on which social relationships are built permits us to begin to build causal connections between some of the phenomena we have documented above. The most clear-cut is the one between family breakdown and child abuse. Martin Daly and Margo Wilson were puzzled by reports of rising rates of child abuse, and suspected the real story had to do with substitute parents. They thought that since 'perhaps the most obvious prediction from a Darwinian view of parental motives is this:

substitute parents will generally tend to care less profoundly for children than natural parents'.[35] The data that Daly and Wilson found from the United States and Canada showed that children were anywhere from ten to over a hundred times more likely to suffer abuse at the hands of substitute rather than natural parents.[36]

Family breakdown is also closely associated with crime more generally, though less than in the case of child abuse. Crime, needless to say, has many environmental causes that have been documented by criminologists over the years, including, among other things, the nature of police enforcement and deterrence. But it also has a biological dimension: crimes are overwhelmingly committed by young males, in virtually all societies around the globe.[37] There is substantial evidence that in addition to being more promiscuous, young males are significantly more aggressive and violent than females and older males, and that this is the result of their underlying psychological make-up rather than culture. Another function of kinship that cuts across virtually all human cultures is the need for a society to control its young males, and the male initiation ceremonies that occur from Polynesia to the US Marine Corps are essentially means by which older males socialize younger ones into the rules of their respective societies. Just as male promiscuity needs to be controlled by the institution of marriage, male aggressiveness needs to be controlled by paternal authority. When this does not happen – when, for example, large numbers of young males are being raised in female-headed families – then a society is, in Daniel Patrick Moynihan's phrase, 'looking for trouble'.[38] According to William Galston and Elaine Kamark:

> The relationship [between family structure and crime] is
> so strong that controlling for family configurations erases
> the relationship between race and crime and between
> low income and crime. This conclusion shows up again
> and again in the literature.[39]

The evidence for the connection is less compelling to James Q. Wilson and Richard Herrnstein, but that is in part because they separate family breakdown into distinct factors like parental attachment, socialization within the family etc., all of which are positively correlated with family structure.[40]

The links between the decline of the nuclear family and the decline of civil society chronicled by Putnam should also be relatively straightforward. Simply looking down his list of organizations that have seen declines in membership – parent-teacher associations, the Red Cross, Scouting and the like – makes clear that many of them were made possible by the uncompensated labour of married women who where outside the paid economy, and that the movement of many of these women into the work force is one important cause of the decline in volunteerism. Married working mothers clearly have problems balancing time requirements between family and job; unpaid work for voluntary organizations tends to be sacrificed early on. This applies doubly so for single parents who, as a group, are poorer and more pressed for time.

Family breakdown also has effects on broader social trust relationships. Social capital within and outside of families are distinct phenomena and can, as noted earlier, be inversely correlated in so-called familistic societies. On the other hand, they can be and very often are positively correlated in countries like the United States, where there are clear empirical links between the stability and quality of family life, and a child's ability to develop co-operative ties with people and groups outside the family. At a minimum, single parenthood or divorce deprives children of access to the father and the father's network of connections in the broader community, as well as undermining trust in an authority figure who is the most obvious role model shaping the child's relationships with other adults.[41] While it is hard to find evidence which supports this directly, it would be surprising if the sharp declines in expressed trust from the survey data were not in some way related to the breaking of primary trust relationships in families.

There are a number of other social indicators that are linked to changes in family relationships that I can only touch on briefly. The decline in the educational achievement of American primary and secondary students has been widely documented and has been the source of endless studies over the past two generations. The causes of this decline are multiple, and the recommendations for how to reverse it are equally diverse. A long series of empirical studies beginning with the famous Coleman Report of the 1960s has indicated, however, that the single factor that can reliably be correlated with educational achievement is not per capita spending on education, standards, the curriculum, computers in the classroom, teacher training, vouchers or any of the other panaceas offered up as public policy solutions, but rather the parents' involvement in their children's education.[42] While educational achievement is not directly linked to family structure, family structure is highly correlated with parental investment and socio-economic status (as will be discussed in the next section), and therefore has consequences for educational achievement as well.[43]

The decline of the nuclear family and the failure to perform the economic and socialization functions it provided appears, then, to be related in varying degrees to many of the social indicators what have turned negative in many developed societies in recent years. Each one of the problems listed here has many differing and complex causes, and it would be foolish to assert that they would all be solved by somehow solving the problem of family cohesion. The arrow of causality runs from family issues towards social structures outside the family, however, the former play an important role in each. It is necessary, then, to understand the reasons for the huge changes in family structure that have taken place throughout most of the developed world since the mid-1960s and the present.

# Causes of changes in family norms

We can begin a discussion of the causes of the decline in nuclear families that took place in the past generation by considering theories of family change that have been put forward by various researchers and groups in what tends to be a rather ideologized debate. Broadly speaking, many on the left argue that family breakdown is related to economic factors like job loss and declining wages, and can be corrected by welfare state protections aimed at reducing poverty. On the right, there are two arguments. The first agrees that family breakdown stems from economic incentives, but believes the welfare state is the cause rather than the cure. The second argues that shifts in norms stem from autonomous cultural or ideological changes – the declining influence of religion, the spread of feminism or the growing legitimacy of individualist doctrines that promote self-gratification and self-realization ahead of community obligations.

In my view, all of these perspectives are flawed. Changes in social norms related to the family are rooted in value change and therefore deeply embedded in broader shifts in culture. But these value changes are, in turn, shaped by economic incentives and technology, the most important of which is the changing ratio of male to female earnings in most post-industrial societies, and birth control.

Let us consider the argument that the changes in family norms described above have been brought about by economic deprivation and by racism and prejudice against minorities. The causal link leading from deprivation to family breakdown led to calls for the United States to enact European-style welfare state protections to guarantee jobs or incomes to poor people, and to subsequent charges that the growing problem of family breakdown was due to the failure of the American welfare state to 'modernize' adequately.[44]

The idea that such large changes in family norms could be brought on by economic deprivation in countries that were wealthier than any other in human history might give one cause for thought. Those favouring this hypothesis argue, of course, that it was the pattern of income distribution rather than per capita income *per se* that was the root of the problem. A casual glance at the comparative data on divorce and illegitimacy rates, however, shows that this cannot possibly be true. If one looks across the OECD, there is no positive correlation between level of welfare benefits and either divorce rates or illegitimacy rates; indeed, there is something of a negative correlation, tending to support the argument advanced by American conservatives that the welfare state is the cause and not the cure for family breakdown. The highest rates of divorce and illegitimacy are found in Scandinavian countries like Sweden and Denmark, which cycle over 70 per cent of their GDPs through the state.[45] This compares to the United States, which cycles only 35–40 per cent of GDP through the federal government.

It is true that the link between family breakdown and poverty is much weaker for countries that have extensive welfare state protections. Poverty rates for single-parent families tend to be higher in the United States than in other OECD countries with larger welfare states, which indicates that various family support and income-maintenance programs appear to have been effective. Many Europeans, seeing data like this, believe that their welfare states have spared them the costs of American-style social problems.

A closer look at the data, however, indicates that the welfare state has not remotely solved the underlying social problem. That is, the state in these cases has simply taken over role of the father, providing mother and children with resources for their protection and upbringing. It is very questionable whether states are adequate substitutes for fathers in terms of socialization. Moreover, it should not be necessary to point out that the European welfare state has run into serious economic problems in the 1990s, producing steadily rising non-accelerating inflationary rates of unemployment in virtually all continental countries. The welfare state does not eliminate the social cost of family breakdown, but rather shifts it from individuals to taxpayers, consumers and the unemployed. The contrast with Japan, which does not suffer from the underlying problem, is instructive and will be explored later.

In the United States, which did much less to protect the poor, there has been a long and tortured debate over the direction of causality between poverty and family breakdown. As noted above, the prevailing view in the 1960s and 1970s after publication of the Moynihan report was that family breakdown was a dependent rather than an independent variable. Typical of the views of that period were those of Herzog and Sudia who maintained that there were no discernible negative social consequences to family breakdown, if one held constant race and income.[46] More data and a new series of detailed studies have changed the consensus substantially; while many social scientists still believe that poverty produces family breakdown, many see a more complex process in which family breakdown is an important independent variable explaining poverty. This would only confirm what we would assume from common sense: that households with only one parent lose economies of scale and can draw on only half as much income and labour compared to those with two (it is actually less than half given lower average earnings for women). They will consequently be able to devote less money, time and energy to their children's education and socialization. This is in fact borne out by the data: following divorce, households experience substantial drops in income, regardless of the parents' pre-divorce socio-economic status.[47]

Conservatives, for their part, have put forward two different arguments to explain family breakdown. The first, associated with Charles Murray, is the mirror image of that of the left: it maintains it is the perverse incentives created by the welfare state itself that explain the rise in family breakdown.[48] The primary American welfare program targeted at poor women, the Depression-era Aid to Families with Dependent Children (AFDC), provided welfare payments only to single mothers and thereby penalized women who married the fathers of their children.[49]

As noted above, the comparative data at first glance gives greater support to the Murray hypothesis than to its left-wing counterpart: high-benefit welfare states like Sweden and Denmark have higher rates of divorce and illegitimacy than low-benefit ones like Japan. There are numerous anomalies, however, beginning with the fact that the United States, which has a substantially lower level of welfare benefits than, say, Germany, has much higher divorce and illegitimacy rates. Detailed studies of welfare benefits in the United States have found similar discrepancies when correlating levels of welfare benefits with illegitimacy either across states (which are allowed to set their own levels of benefits) or across time.[50] One analyst suggests that perhaps 15 per cent of family breakdown in the United States can be attributed to AFDC and other welfare programs.[51]

The other, more common conservative argument

maintains that family breakdown and its correlates is due to a massive cultural shift that took place at the beginning of the 1960s. This cultural shift saw earlier norms of marital fidelity, self-sacrifice, duty towards community obligations and respect for authority replaced by an emphasis on individualism, personal gratification, independence on the part of women and rights over duties in an individual's relationship to family, neighbourhood, workplace and country. There is an abundance of more detailed theories as to why this cultural shift took place. Some relate it to the decline of religion and what is believed to be the inevitable secularization that takes place as societies modernize. Others relate it to particular events that took place at the time, such as the assassination of John F. Kennedy, the war in Vietnam or the series of scandals that engulfed American presidents from the late 1960s onwards.

It should be obvious to anyone living in this period that there has been a massive cultural shift in many post-industrial societies to a greater emphasis on individualism rather than community.[52] Ronald Inglehart's massive and long-running World Values Survey at the University of Michigan, as well as Daniel Yankelovich's opinion surveys, have documented empirically the nature of the value shift that has happened across a wide variety of cultures.[53] The question, however, is whether this value shift was truly autonomous, or whether it was in turn shaped by other, more basic socio-economic forces that make it to some extent a dependent variable.

There is good reason to treat the view that the Great Disruption was caused by an autonomous shift in values with some caution. Everything we know about cultural variables is that they tend to change very slowly when compared to other kinds of factors, such as shifts in economic conditions, public policies or ideology. In those cases where cultural variables have changed quickly, such as in rapidly modernizing Third World societies, cultural change is clearly being driven by socio-economic change and is therefore not an autonomous factor. So with the Great Disruption: it is hard to believe that people throughout the developed world simply decided to change their attitudes towards such elemental issues as marriage, divorce, child-rearing, authority and community so as to completely alter the nature of the family in the space of two or three decades. Those explanations that link changes in cultural variables to specific events in American history like Vietnam, Watergate or the counterculture of the 1960s betray an even greater provincialism: why then were social norms disrupted in other societies from Sweden and Iceland to New Zealand and Spain?

To explain the Great Disruption, we need to look for large-scale social changes that correlate with it both geographically – to account for the varying levels of disruption in different societies – and also ones that would correlate with it over time, to explain why the disruption began in the 1960s rather than a generation earlier or later.

# Birth control and working women

I noted earlier that human kinship can be understood as a tacit trade of fertility for economic resources, and that while the forms of kinship may vary, its objective does not. Females tend to be much more selective in choosing their partners and interested in long-term commitments because the consequences of making a mistake – an unwanted child – are much more severe for them than for males. Hence the development of powerful social norms surrounding marriage in all cultures. In the United States and other Western countries, men were required to turn over, in effect, a substantial part of their lifetime earnings to their wives and children, reflecting the seriousness of the stakes involved.

The single most important co-operative social norm that has changed since then is that males are expected to live up to their end of the marriage bargain. There is evidence that as late as the 1950s in the United States, over 60 per cent of all brides were pregnant at the altar and their bridegrooms coerced into marriage (usually through the efforts of the girl's male relatives).[54] Premarital sex was, evidently, quite common among young people in those years, but the social consequences were mitigated by the norm of male responsibility.

What accounts for the breakdown of this norm and the bargain that rested on it? Two very important changes occurred sometime during the early post-war period that account for many of the phenomena constituting the Great Disruption. The first involved advances in medical technology - i.e. birth control and abortion – that for the first time permitted women to control their own reproductive cycles. The second was the movement of women into the paid labour force in most industrialized countries, and the steady rise in their incomes – hourly, median or lifetime – relative to men over the next thirty

Figure 1.12: 'Shotgun' marriage rates, US

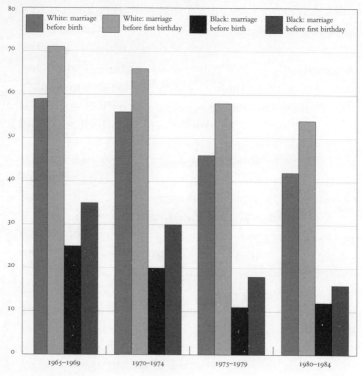

years.

The significance of birth control was not that it lowered fertility, since fertility rates have been on the decline in many societies prior to the widespread availability of birth control or abortion.[55] Indeed, if the effect of birth control is to reduce the number of unwanted pregnancies, it is hard to explain why its advent should have been accompanied by a rise in the rate of abortions,[56] or why use of birth control is positively correlated with illegitimacy across the OECD.[57]

The main impact of the Pill and the sexual revolution that followed was to dramatically alter calculations about the risks of sex, and thereby to change male, rather than female, behaviour. The reason that the rates of birth control use, abortions and illegitimacy all increased in tandem is that a fourth rate – the number of shotgun marriages – declined substantially at the same time (see FIGURE 1.12 opposite). Since the Pill permitted women for the first time to have sex without worrying about economic consequences, men felt liberated from norms requiring them to look after the women they had got pregnant.

The second factor altering male behaviour is the entry of women into the labour force. That female incomes should be related to family breakdown is an argument associated most closely with economist Gary Becker.[58] Increasing female earnings make it possible, of course, for women to support themselves and their children without husbands. The more subtle consequence, however, was to further weaken the norm of male responsibility. This reinforced, in turn, the need for women to arm themselves with job skills so as not to be dependent on decreasingly reliable husbands.

There is considerable empirical evidence that Becker is right about the importance, to put it crudely, of husbands as economic commodities in marriage markets. FIGURE 1.13, overleaf, shows the changing rate of male v. female labour force participation in the United States between 1960 and 1995. Not only does female participation jump from 35 per cent to 55 per cent in this thirty-five year period, but male participation actually drops from 79 per cent to 71 per cent.

**Figure 1.13: Labour force participation by sex, US, 1960–95**

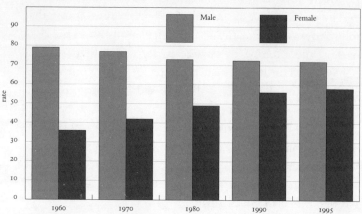

**Figure 1.14: Male–female median incomes, US, 1947–95**

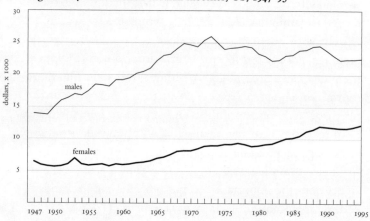

FIGURE 1.14 shows changes in male and female median incomes in the United States between 1947 and 1995. It is interesting to note that male median incomes, after dropping slightly in the immediate post-war period, rise steadily up

**Figure 1.15: Female–male ratio of median income, US, 1947–95**

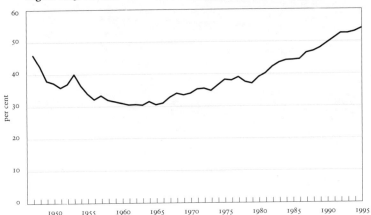

through the late 1960s, after which they stagnate. Indeed, male real median incomes were higher in the early 1970s than they are today. Female incomes, on the other hand, after dropping slightly in the late 1940s as female workers left wartime employment, have risen steadily from the early 1960s to the present day.

FIGURE 1.15, above, plots the change in the ratio of female to male median incomes over this same time period. I noted earlier that the immediate post-war period was one in which divorce rates fell, fertility rose and family stability actually improved. It is probably more than a coincidence that the female-male median income ratio actually shifted in favour of men in this period. On the other hand, the ratio turned sharply in favour of women beginning around 1967. Again, as we have noted, 1967 is a good starting date for the Great Disruption.

The ratio of female to male earnings also does a great deal

**Figure 1.16: Female–male median income ratios, blacks and all US workers, 1948–95**

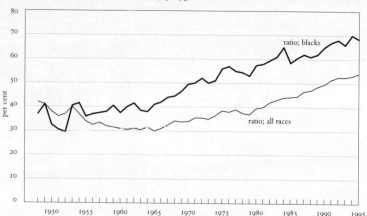

to explain the crisis of the African-American family. FIGURE 1.16, above, compares changes in the female-male median income ratio for American blacks compared to all American workers from 1951 to 1995. The black ratio shifts much more rapidly in favour of black women than does the ratio for all races. In the immediate post-war period, the ratios are roughly the same for blacks as for all Americans; by the end of the period, black women have gained on black men by more than fifteen percentage points than the population as a whole. This chart probably understates the difference, since it only measures people with incomes. Black male rates of unemployment relative to female rates are higher than comparable rates for whites, further accentuating the relative disadvantages of black men.

What happens if we broaden our survey to other OECD countries? FIGURE 1.17, opposite, plots changes in female labour force participation against changes in the divorce rate

**Figure 1.17: Changes to divorce rates v. female labour force participation**

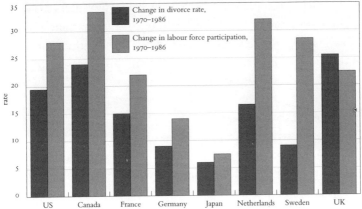

**Figure 1.18: Illegitimacy v. female labour force participation**

between approximately 1970 and 1990 for eight selected OECD countries. The chart indicates that there is a broad correlation between women moving into the labour force and changes in divorce rates. FIGURE 1.18, above, plots changes in female labour force participation against the 1993 illegitimacy rate for nine OECD countries. The fit here is slightly less good than for divorces, but once again there is a broad correlation between female labour force participation and change in family structure. In both cases the Netherlands and Sweden are outliers.

### The special case of Japan

In the OECD world, Japan is an interesting case because up to this point it has not experienced the Great Disruption, despite the fact that today it has the world's second highest per capita income. As indicated in the previous charts, Japanese divorce rates have edged up slightly over the past two generations, while illegitimacy rates have actually fallen. Crime rates, low to begin with by OECD standards, have also fallen over the same period, as have other social deviance indicators.

The reason why the Japanese have escaped the disruptions experienced by other developed countries is clearly shown by the data. While Japanese rates of female labour force participation are not unusually low for an OECD country, they mask a much greater economic disparity between men and women. A woman's decision either to remain unmarried or to raise a family without the benefit of a husband depends not simply on her having a job, but also on her prospects for being self-supporting over a lifetime. A great deal of Japanese female employment is temporary, or else represents a form of underemployment. That is, young women will enter the labour force after secondary school or college with the expectation that they will work only until they get married.

Figure 1.19: Female–male earnings ratios, selected OECD countries

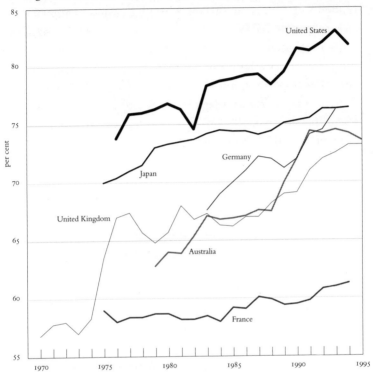

If one looks at the ratio of female to male median incomes in Japan over the past forty years, not only do we find that it is significantly lower than for other OECD countries, but that it has increased in favour of women only marginally (see FIGURE 1.19, above). Japanese labour laws permit wage discrimination in favour of men – especially men with families – and divorce laws have historically been biased towards men. The economic prospects of a single woman raising a family in Japan are decidedly worse than in the United States, Sweden, Britain or other European countries.

Finally, it should be noted that the Pill was only legalized in Japan in 1996. As in certain former communist countries, the Japanese have typically used abortion rather than birth control to regulate fertility. However, unlike a country such as Romania, abortion in Japan carries with it a considerable social stigma. Japanese women, in short, have had much less control over their reproductive cycles than their Western counterparts, which reinforces the male norm of responsibility towards women.

The Japanese case indicates that economic modernization does not inevitably lead to the kinds of changes in social norms that have been happening in Western Europe and North America. Despite greater opportunities for women to move into the workforce, based on changes in the nature of work itself in post-industrial societies, the Japanese have kept a number of discriminatory measures in place that have made it less likely that women will do so. Whether Japan can continue such policies remains to be seen. Due to declining fertility rates over the past two generations, Japan faces a labour force that in 1996 declined in absolute numbers for the first time. Japan's population will continue to decline (unless there is an unexpected increase in fertility) through much of the next century, until it is perhaps half of today's levels by the second half of the century. The ageing of Japan's population and the declining ratio of working age to the retired population creates a huge future social security liability. One method of mitigating this situation is to allow more foreign workers into the country, something that Japan has resisted strongly up to now. The other possibility is to encourage more women to enter the workforce, not just prior to marriage but throughout their working lives.

The situation in Japan also sheds interesting light on the 'Asian values' debate that has taken place on both sides of the Pacific in recent years. Asian leaders like former Singaporean prime minister Lee Kuan Yew and Malaysian prime minister Mahatir bin Muhammed have both argued that Asian economic performance has been aided by distinctively Asian cultural values.[59] They have pointed to the kinds of social deviance indicators outlined above, particularly in the United States, in building their case that the Western cultural model is one they do not want to follow. While this is not stated explicitly by most participants in this debate, the core value that differentiates many Asian societies from those in the West concerns the status of women. The reason why Asian societies, beginning with Japan, have been able to avoid the kinds of social problems facing North America and Europe is because they have more strongly resisted female equality.

## Social norms and economic incentives

By arguing that the Great Disruption had causes that were ultimately economic and technological, I do not mean to suggest that values, whether derived from religion, traditional or popular culture, are not important in changing the way that people relate to one another in families and in civil society. The declining importance of physical labour in a modern economy and innovations in birth control and technology have both occurred in Japan as well as the United States. Yet the Japanese case shows that a society with different cultural priorities can deal with these same economic changes in a very different manner, at least in the short run. In any event, values are the critical mediating force between changes in economic conditions and individual decisions.

But values need to be put in a broader economic and biological context. Evolutionary psychology suggests that male altruism towards offspring, while rooted in biology, is more the product of socially constructed norms than female altruism. From the standpoint of reproductive strategy, it makes adaptive sense for males to mate with as many females as possible and to father children through multiple partners. The fact that human males with high status and/or wealth have done this readily in cultures from China to Turkey to present-day corporate America suggests that this drive is still very much with us (the difference being, of course, that American corporate executives have their wives and children serially rather than simultaneously as in the case of Ottoman pashas or Chinese Mandarins).

It is easy to see how the change in economic conditions in recent decades has altered the norm of male responsibility. With birth control and easier abortion, the economic consequences of sex have declined dramatically for women, so they can afford to be much less selective in their choice of partners. With the movement of women into the paid labour force, abandonment of a wife and children does not have the same dramatic negative consequences as it once did. Many women prize the greater freedom that economic independence brings – hence the feminist movement – and their assertion of independence releases men from the norm of family responsibility. Males do not have to be persuaded to behave less than responsibly towards their families; there are plenty of biological forces pushing them in this direction as it is. The growth of male irresponsibility then reinforces the female drive for independence: even if a girl wanted to grow up to be a dependent homemaker today, she would be ill-advised not to equip herself with job skills, given that her marriage partner is more likely than not to either end up abandoning her and her children, or to have difficulties providing a family income. When these tendencies towards greater independence on the part of both men and women are reinforced by a general Western culture that celebrates individualism, and by a specifically American culture that denigrates the importance of virtually all inherited social duties and obligations, it is easy to see why the United States ends up with a serious degree of family breakdown and declining levels of social capital.

# Part 2: Technology Hierarchy and Networks

# Economic uses of social capital

The modern capitalist economy uses, depletes and replenishes social capital. Neo-classical economists understand the importance of co-operative social norms to the economy, and have an elaborate theory to explain how selfish rational agents come to co-operate with one another. Economists also understand institutionally constructed norms: their theory provides guidelines for evaluating what is efficiency-enhancing or efficiency-retarding state behaviour. What economists have a harder time accepting is the importance of what can be labelled 'exogenously constructed norms', that is, norms affecting economic behaviour that are exogenous to the economic system, originating from sources like religion and culture.

There is, of course, a substantial body of literature on the impact of exogenously generated norms on the economy under the general heading of culture and economics. The *locus classicus* for this type of analysis was Max Weber's *The Protestant Ethic and the Spirit of Capitalism* (1930), which argued that Puritanism was a system of beliefs exogenous to the market economy, but which nonetheless had a critical role in making the Industrial Revolution possible. In *Trust* (1995), I gave a number of examples of ways in which social capital shapes the contemporary global economy, for example, by making family firms the vehicle of economic expansion in places like central Italy, Hong Kong and Taiwan.

I do not wish to rehash these arguments here, except to underline the point that exogenous norms were never intended to constitute a *primary* explanation for economic growth. The standard economic growth models that look to factors like labour, capital, resources, technology and macroeconomic policy will always constitute the primary explanation for why certain economies prosper while others do not. All of these models, however, leave large residuals in the degree to which they can adequately account for observed growth, and I believe that cultural factors play an important role in accounting for some of that residual. We may never be able to specify precisely how much of a role they play because of the measurement problems alluded to in Part 1. As I argued in *Trust*, the primary impact of social capital on the particular economies I studied seemed to be less on aggregate growth itself than on sector specialization and the role of the state in guiding the economy.

Many social scientists will accept the importance of exogenously generated norms in the capitalist economy, and many further believe that over time the latter plays a role in depleting the social capital that has been built up through non-economic means. There is a significant and interesting literature on the 'cultural contradictions of capitalism', which argues that capitalist development ultimately undermines itself by producing insufficient norms, or else by producing norms at odds with those necessary for the operation of markets and innovation. Perhaps the most famous exponent of this view was Joseph Schumpeter, who argued in *Capitalism, Socialism and Democracy* that over time capitalism tended to produce a class of élites that was hostile to the very forces that had made their lives possible, and that they would eventually seek to replace market economies with socialist ones.[60] Daniel Bell and others have written about the problems of affluence in undermining the work ethic and other kinds of norms necessary to the capitalist order.[61] It is a staple of the contemporary literature about corporate lay-offs and downsizing that the global economy has become an enemy of community by disrupting families, localities and the loyalties that at one time pervaded the workplace.[62]

The problem with this literature, apart from the fact that capitalism has not yet collapsed or otherwise undermined itself, is that it is extremely one-sided. That is, it sees capitalism as a destructive, disruptive force that breaks apart traditional loyalties and obligations, but fails to see the ways in which capitalism also creates order and builds new norms to replace the ones it destroyed. Indeed, it may be possible that capitalism is a net creator of norms. What I intend to argue in the remainder of this second part is that there are reasons for thinking social capital and informal norms will become even more important as we move from an industrial to a post-industrial or information age economy, and as the complexity and technological level of an economy grows. Whether these norms will actually be produced to meet this demand, and how this will come about, is a separate subject that I will deal with in Part 3.

# Markets, hierarchies and networks

There is by now a substantial literature, produced primarily by management specialists, on the rise of the network as an intermediate form of organization between traditional markets and hierarchies.[63] There is a general consensus that large, hierarchical organizations are in trouble. In an article

**Figure 2.1: Traditional hierarchy**

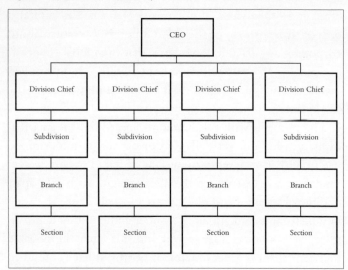

often-cited, Malone and Yates argued that the advent of cheap and ubiquitous information technology should reduce the transaction costs involved in market relationships, and thereby reduce the incentive to create managerial hierarchies.[64] Indeed, many apostles of the information revolution have seen the rise of the Internet not simply as a useful new communications technology, but as the harbinger of an entirely new, non-hierarchical form of organization uniquely adapted to the requirements of a complex, information-intensive economic world.

Much of the prevailing literature understands the shift that is occurring in terms of formal organization. FIGURE 2.1, above, outlines the classic pyramidal shape of a hierarchical Taylorite organization, while FIGURE 2.2, opposite, shows the

**Figure 2.2: The Flat Organisation**

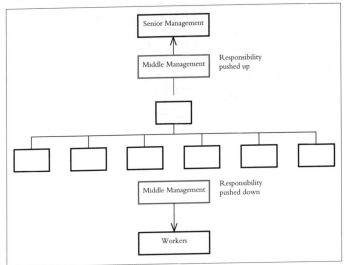

consequences of organizational 'flattening.' The flat organization remains ultimately a centralized and hierarchical one; all that has been changed is the number of management layers intervening between the top and bottom. Flat organizations create enlarged spans of control; properly executed, they should not overburden senior managers with micromanagement responsibilities, but rather should push down authority to the lower levels of the organization.

Sociologists have, of course, used the concept of 'networks' since at least the days of Georg Simmel, and at times express annoyance that business school professors are now reinventing the wheel. The definition of a network commonly used by sociologists, however, is extremely broad

**Figure 2.3: Networks: Radical decentralisation**

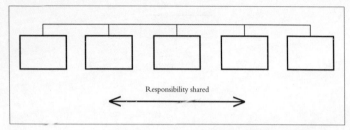

Responsibility shared

and encompasses both markets and hierarchies as they are understood by economists.[65] There is a striking lack of precision in the use of the term 'network' among the management specialists, however. While networks are commonly understood to be different from hierarchies, it is often not clear how they differ from markets. Indeed, Thomas Malone did not use the term 'network' when he originally talked about the decline of hierarchies; co-ordination would be performed by classical market mechanisms.[66] Some people treat the network as a category of formal organization in which there is no formal source of sovereign authority (see FIGURE 2.3, above). Others understand it to be a set of informal relationships or alliances between organizations, each of which may be hierarchical but which are related to one another through vertical contractual relationships (see FIGURE 2.4, opposite). Japanese *keiretsu* groups, alliances of small family firms in Central Italy and Boeing's relationships with its suppliers are equally understood to be networks.

The social capital perspective, in my view, gives us ground for defining a network in a more precise way to permit us to understand what its economic function really is. In this view,

**Figure 2.4: Networks: Informal alliances**

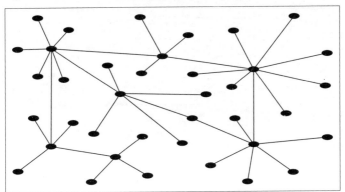

a network does not define a type of formal organization, but rather a moral relationship of trust. So, a more precise definition would be:

> A network is a group of individual agents that share *informal* norms or values beyond those necessary for ordinary market transactions.

The norms and values encompassed under this definition can extend from the simple norm of reciprocity shared between two friends, to the complex value systems created by organized religions. A non-governmental organization like Amnesty International or the National Organization for Women also achieves co-ordinated action on the basis of shared values; as in the case of friends or members of a religious organization, the behaviour of the organization's individual members cannot be explained on the grounds of economic self-interest alone. A society like the United States

Figure 2.5: Networks of trust overlap

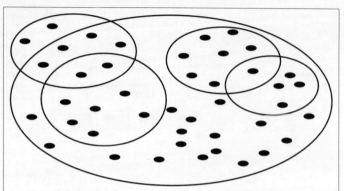

is characterized by a dense, complex and overlapping set of networks (see FIGURE 2.5).

There are two features to note in this definition. A network is different from a market insofar as networks are defined by their shared norms and values. This means that economic exchange within a network will be conducted on a different basis than economic transactions in a market. A purist might argue that even market transactions require *some* shared norms (the willingness, for example, to engage in exchange rather than violence); but the norms required for economic exchange are relatively minimal. Exchange can occur between people who do not know or like one another, who speak different languages; indeed, it can occur anonymously between agents who never know each other's identities. Exchange among members of a network is different: the shared norms give them a superordinate purpose that distorts the market relationship. Hence members of the same family, or of the Sierra Club or an

**Figure 2.6: A Corporate Culture**

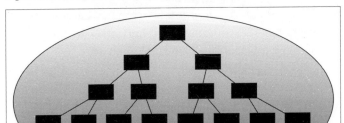

ethnic rotating-credit association, sharing as they do certain common norms (if only a norm of reciprocity based on past exchange) do not deal with each other the way that agents meeting in a marketplace do. They are much more willing to confer benefits, for example, without expecting immediate benefits in return; while they may expect long-term individual returns, the exchange relationship is not dependent on a careful cost-benefit calculation as it is in a market transaction.

On the other hand, a network is different from a hierarchy because it is based on shared *informal* norms and not on a formal authority relationship. Understood in this sense, a network can coexist with a formal hierarchy. Members of a formal hierarchy do not have to share norms or values with one another beyond the wage contracts that define their membership; formal organizations, however, can be overlaid with informal networks of various sorts, based on patronage, ethnicity, or a common corporate culture. FIGURE 2.6

illustrates a formal hierarchical organization, all of whose members share a common corporate culture. While networks can coexist with formal organizations, they can, at one extreme, also replace formal organizations.

It should be clear that when networks are overlaid on top of formal organizations, the results are not necessarily beneficial, and indeed can be the source of a good deal of organizational dysfunction. Everyone is familiar with patronage networks, based on kinship, friendship, love or some such factor. Members of such a network share important norms and values with one another (particularly reciprocity) that they do not share with other members of the organization. FIGURE 2.7, opposite, illustrates a patronage network superimposed over an organization with a common corporate culture. Within the patronage network, information passes readily, but its outer boundaries constitute a membrane through which information passes much less readily. Patronage networks are problematic in organizations because their structure is not obvious to those outside of them and they often subvert formal authority relationships. Common ethnicity may facilitate trust and exchange among members of the same ethnic group, but it inhibits exchange between members of different groups. Often, the bonds of reciprocity between members of a network are undertaken for non-economic reasons and stand in the way of economic rationality – for example, when a boss is unwilling to criticize or fire an incompetent subordinate because the latter is a protégé or personal friend.

The other problem with informal networks is that there is an inverse proportion between the strength of the values or

**Figure 2.7: A Patronage Network**

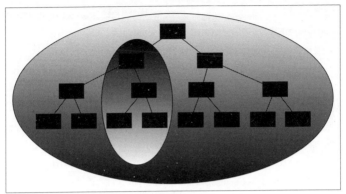

norms linking the community (and therefore the degree of co-ordination they can achieve) and their openness to people, ideas and influences from outside the network. Being a member of the US Marine Corps or the Mormon Church involves much more than membership of a formal organization; one is also socialized into a strong and distinctive 'organizational culture' that creates a high degree of internal solidarity and potential for co-ordinated activity. On the other hand, the cultural gap between a Marine and a civilian, or a Mormon and non-Mormon, is much greater than for organizations with lesser degrees of moral relatedness. The impermeability of the communal walls around such groups can often make them intolerant, inbred, slow to adapt and oblivious to new ideas. Following Granovetter, there has been a large amount of literature produced on the importance of 'weak ties' on the effectiveness of informational networks.[67] It is the deviant individuals straddling different communities who are often

71

responsible for bringing in heterodox ideas that are ultimately necessary if the group is to successfully adapt to changes in its environment.

Networks, understood as informal ethical relationships, are therefore associated with phenomena like nepotism, favoritism, intolerance, inbreeding and non-transparent, personalistic arrangements. Networks in this sense are as old as human communities themselves, and in many respects were the dominant form of social relationship in many pre-modern societies. In some sense, many of the institutions we associate with modernity, such as contract, rule of law, constitutionalism and the institutional separation of powers were all designed to counteract the defects of informal network relationships. Indeed, Weber and other interpreters of modernity argued its essence was the replacement of informal authority with law and transparent institutions.[68]

So why is it, then, that anyone should believe that human organizations will in the future move away from formal hierarchies and toward informal networks? In fact, it is highly doubtful that formal hierarchies are about to disappear anytime soon; networks will become important to the extent that they will exist in conjunction with formal hierarchies. But why should informal networks not wither away altogether? One answer has to do with the problems of co-ordination under conditions of increasing economic complexity.

# Changing methods of coordination

As Kenneth Arrow has pointed out, an organization can be seen in very general terms as a means of achieving co-ordinated action in situations where the price system has failed, either as a result of externalities or because the high transaction costs of co-ordination through the price system makes hierarchical co-ordination more efficient.[69]

The importance of social capital in a hierarchical organization can be understood in terms of the economics of information. A hierarchy exists in order to co-ordinate the flow of material resources in a production process. While the flow of material product is determined by the formal structure of authority, the flow of information proceeds in a much more complex fashion. As is well known, information is different from other kinds of products insofar as it is subject to increasing returns in use, and also to sharply declining costs: once created, further copies are essentially free. This means that, in theory, any information generated within an organization should optimally flow freely to all other parts of the organization where it can be of use. Since the organization in principle owns the property rights to all information generated by its workers, there should be no transaction costs involved in the transfer of those property rights from one part of the organization to another. There is a substantial business school literature today on strategies for 'mining' the knowledge that exists in a firm but is under-utilized by it.

The reason information does not flow freely and is typically under-utilized has to do, of course, with various principal-agent problems within hierarchical organizations. Organizations are typically thought of by economists as bundles of agency contracts, and the central managerial problem is to align individual incentives with organizational incentives so that the agents work in the principal's best interests. This frequently fails to happen for a number of reasons. For one thing, individual and organizational interests are at times in conflict: a middle manager who discovers a new application of information technology or a new plan for flattening the managerial structure that will eliminate his own job has no incentive to implement this discovery.[70] In other cases where outputs are difficult to measure, monitoring individual performance for the sake of individualized incentives becomes prohibitively expensive.

Thus, while it is in the organization's overall interest to promote the free flow of information, it is often not in the individual interests of the various agents within the hierarchy to allow it to do so. Information, as the saying goes, is power, and the granting or withholding of information becomes one of the principle means by which various agents within an organization seek to maximize their power relative to other agents. Everyone who has worked in a hierarchical organization knows that there is a constant struggle going on between superiors and subordinates to control information; the withholding of information is frequently a subordinate's most important source of leverage over a superior.

In addition to principal-agent problems, organizations suffer from other dis-economies of scale related to information processing. Many transaction costs are internal to organizations, and are created by the difficulties in passing information up and down a large hierarchy. We have all worked in hierarchical organizations in which Department x does not know what Department y on the next floor is doing. Ideally, information ought to be processed as close to its source within the organization as possible. Some decisions require higher-level monitoring, and therefore the transaction costs of that monitoring are higher; in other cases, organizations assign monitoring responsibilities unnecessarily, incorrectly or inefficiently. This, in a sense, was the central economic failure of socialism; as von Mises and Hayek have pointed out, centralization of economic decision-making created information processing problems of 'unmanageable complexity'.[71]

The formality of hierarchies can also create problems in dealing with complex information. Management through a hierarchy usually entails the creation of a system of formal rules and standard operating procedures – the essence of Weberian bureaucracy. Formal rules become problematic when decisions have to be made on the basis of information that is complex or hard to measure and evaluate. In labour markets, advertising and listings of formal job requirements are used to match supply and demand for simple, low-skill jobs,[72] informal networks take over when universities or firms need to hire hotshot economists or software engineers, because their skills and performance are much harder to define in formal terms.

Finally, hierarchies can be less adaptive. Formalized systems of control are much less flexible than informal ones; when environmental conditions change, they are often more visible to the lower levels of an organization than to the higher levels. Hence over-centralization can be a particular liability in areas of rapid environmental change, such as the present-day information technology industry.

The reason that networks, defined as groups sharing informal norms and values, are important, is that they provide alternative conduits for the flow of information through an organization. Friends do not typically stand on their intellectual property rights when sharing information with each other, and therefore do not incur transaction costs. Friendships thus facilitate the free flow of information within the organization. Nor do friends usually spend a lot of time strategizing over how to maximize their relative power positions *vis-à-vis* each other. Someone in marketing knows someone in production and tells them over lunch about customer complaints concerning product quality, thereby bypassing the formal hierarchy and moving information to the place where it is most useful more quickly. A corporate culture ideally provides an individual worker with a group as well as individual identity, encouraging effort towards group ends that again facilitate information flow within the organization.

Social capital is also critical to the management of highly skilled workers manipulating complex, diffuse, tacit or knowledge and processes that are hard-to-communicate. Organizations from universities to engineering, accounting and architectural firms generally do not try to manage their professional staff through detailed bureaucratic work rules or standard operating procedures. Such workers are usually trusted to be self-managing on the basis of internalized professional standards. A doctor presumably will not do just anything to a patient if someone pays him enough; he has taken an oath to serve the patient's interests rather than his own. Professional education is consequently a major source of social capital in any advanced, post-industrial society and provides the basis for decentralized, flat organization.

I would argue that social capital is important to certain sectors and certain forms of complex production precisely because exchange based on informal norms can avoid the internal transaction costs of large hierarchical organizations, as well as the external transaction costs of arm's length market transactions. The need for informal, norm-based exchange becomes more important as goods and services become more complex, difficult to evaluate and differentiated. The increasing importance of social capital can be seen in the shift from low-trust to high-trust manufacturing, among other places.

# From low-trust to high-trust production

The Taylorite factory, as implemented in Henry Ford's Highland Park facility and countless other twentieth century large manufacturing facilities, was a hierarchical organization characterized by a high degree of formality. That is, there was an extensive division of labour mandated and controlled through a centralized, bureaucratic hierarchy, which laid down a large number of formal rules for how the individual members of the organization were to behave. Taylorism contained an implicit premise that there were economies of scale in managerial intelligence, and that an organization could operate more efficiently if the firm's intelligence was segregated in a white collar managerial hierarchy rather than distributed throughout the organization.

In such a system there was no need for trust, social capital or informal social norms: every worker was told where to stand, how to move his arms and legs, when to take breaks and was not generally expected to display the slightest degree of creativity or judgment. Workers were motivated by purely individual incentives, whether by rewards or punishments, and were readily interchangeable with one another. Reacting to this system through the unions, the blue collar labour force demanded formal guarantees of their rights and the narrowest possible specification of duties. Hence the rise of job-control unionism and labour contracts that were as thick as telephone books.[73]

Taylorism was an effective means – perhaps the only means – of co-ordinating the activities of a low-skill industrial labour force. In the first two decades of the century, half of Ford's blue collar workers were first generation immigrants who could not speak English, and as late as the 1950s 80 per cent did not have any secondary education. But Taylorism ran into all of the problems of large, hierarchical organizations, with slow decision-making, inflexible workplace rules and an inability to adapt to new circumstances.

There is a certain parallel between the Taylorite factory and the concept of the modern, rational, bureaucratic state. And it is no accident that today the Taylorite factory is undergoing rapid change just as the modern state appears to have reached its limits. The limits of Taylorism have been discussed extensively in the existing literature, and it is not necessary to detail them here, nor to describe the flatter, less hierarchical forms of management that have replaced it. The point I want to stress here is that the move from a hierarchical Taylorite organization to a flat or networked one involves offloading the co-ordination function from formal bureaucratic rules to informal social norms. Authority does not disappear in a flat or networked organization; rather, it is internalized in a way that permits self-organization and self-management.

A lean or just-in-time automobile factory is an example of a flat, post-Fordist organization. In terms of formal authority, many of the functions previously assigned to white collar middle managers have now been undertaken by blue collar assembly-line workers themselves acting in teams. It is the factory-floor work force itself that manages day-to-day scheduling, machine setup, work discipline and quality control. The degree to which power has been moved down to the bottom layer of the organization is symbolized by the famous cord at each workstation in Toyota's Takaoka assembly plant, which allows each individual blue collar worker to stop the entire assembly line if he or she sees a problem in the production process. The cord constitutes what game theorists would call a 'unit veto', by which each actor can sabotage the entire group's effort. It is obvious that this kind of authority can be safely delegated only under certain conditions: the blue collar work force has to be adequately trained to be able to undertake the management skills formerly performed by white collar middle managers, and they have to have a sense of responsibility to use their power to further the group rather than individual ends. The post-Fordist factory requires, in other words, a higher degree of trust and social capital than the Taylorite workplace with its comprehensive workplace rules.

# Regionalism and social networks

As any number of studies have indicated, lean manufacturing has succeeded in improving productivity in the worldwide automobile industry by substantial margins, while at the same time improving product quality. [74] The reason for this is that information is processed much closer to its source: if a door panel from a subcontractor doesn't fit properly, the worker assigned to bolt it to the chassis has both the authority and the incentive to see that the problem is fixed, rather than letting the information get lost while traveling up and down a long managerial hierarchy.

I will provide one further example of where social capital is critical to implementing a flat or networked form of organization, which is the American information technology industry. Silicon Valley might at first glance seem to be a low trust, low social capital part of the American economy, where competition rather than co-operation is the norm, and where efficiency arises out of the workings of rational utility-maximizers meeting in impersonal markets as described by the neo-classical model. Firms are numerous, small and constantly fissioning from one another; they bubble up and die as a result of cutthroat competition. Employment is insecure, lifetime employment and loyalty to a given company is unheard-of. The relatively unregulated nature of the information technology industry, combined with well-developed venture capital markets, permits a high degree of entrepreneurial individualism.

This picture of unbridled competitive individualism is belied, however, by any number of more detailed sociological studies of the actual nature of technological development in the Valley, such as Annalee Saxenian's *Regional Advantage*.[75] In assessing the role of social capital in a modern economy, it is important to note that it does not have to manifest itself within the boundaries of individual companies, or be embodied in practices like lifetime employment.[76] Saxenian contrasts the performance of Silicon Valley with Boston's Route 128, and notes that one important reason for the former's success had to do with the Valley's different culture. Saxenian makes clear that beneath the surface of apparently unbridled individualistic competition was a wide array of social networks linking individuals in different companies in the semiconductor and computer businesses. These social networks had a variety of sources, including common education background (e.g. getting an electrical engineering degree from Berkeley or Stanford), common employment histories (many key players in the semiconductor industry like Robert Noyce and Andy Grove worked closely with one another in the early days of the industry at Fairchild Semiconductor), or else absorbed the communal norms of the Bay Area counterculture of the late 1960s and 1970s.

Informal networks are critical to technology development for a number of reasons. A great deal of knowledge is tacit and cannot be easily reduced to a commodity that can be bought and sold in an intellectual property market. The enormous complexity of both the underlying technologies and the systems-integration problem mean that even the largest technology firms will not be able to generate adequate technical knowledge in-house. While technology is transferred between firms through mergers, acquisitions, cross-licensing and formal partnerships, the literature on technology development in Silicon Valley stresses the informal nature of a great deal of the R&D work there. According to Saxenian:

> The informal socializing that grew out of these quasi-familial relationships supported the ubiquitous practices of collaboration and sharing of information among local producers. The Wagon Wheel bar in Mountain View, a popular watering hole where engineers met to exchange ideas and gossip, has been termed 'the fountainhead of the semiconductor industry' ... By all accounts, these informal conversations were pervasive and served as an important source of up-to-date information about competitors, customers, markets, and technologies ... In an industry characterized by rapid technological change and intense competition, such informal communication was often of more value than more conventional but less timely forums such as industry journals.[77]

She argues that the proprietary attitudes of a Route 128 firm like Digital Equipment proved to be a liability; unable ultimately to be a self-sufficient vertically-integrated producer of technology, it lacked the informal links and trust necessary to share technology with rivals.

That these technology networks had an ethical and social dimension critical to their economic function is clear from Saxenian's comment that:

> Local engineers recognize that the quality of the

feedback and information obtained through their networks depends upon the credibility and trustworthiness of the information provider. This sort of quality is only assured with individuals with whom you share common backgrounds and work experiences.[78]

These shared professional and personal norms thus constituted an important form of social capital.

Other writers have analyzed the growth of so-called 'communities of practice' in other areas of technology development. That is, individual engineers working on the development of a specific technology tend to share information with one another on the basis of mutual respect and trust. The communities that emerge are *sui generis*; while they may be based on common educational or employment backgrounds, they frequently span the boundaries of individual organizations and areas of professional specialization.

It should be noted that these informal networks are probably more important in the information technology industry than in other sectors. In the chemical/pharmaceutical industry, where a large revenue stream can rest on the knowledge of a single molecule, companies are understandably more cautious about sharing their proprietary knowledge. Information technology, by contrast, is what Don Kash calls complex, involving the integration of a large number of highly complex product and process technologies. The likelihood that a given part of proprietary intellectual property shared with a potential competitor will lead to direct losses is relatively small.

The social capital produced by such informal social networks permits Silicon Valley to achieve scale economies in R&D not possible in large, vertically-integrated firms. Much has been written about the co-operative character of Japanese firms, and the way in which technology is shared among members of a *keiretsu* network. In a certain sense, the whole of Silicon Valley can been seen as a single large network organization, that can tap expertise and specialized skills unavailable to even the largest vertically-integrated Japanese electronics firms and their *keiretsu* networks.[79]

The importance of social capital to technology development has some paradoxical results. One is that geographical proximity remains important – perhaps even more important than previously. A number of observers have noted that despite advances in communications and transportation technology, a number of industries, and particularly high-tech R&D, remain highly concentrated in particular geographical locations. If information can now be readily shared over electronic networks, why is there not further geographical dispersal of industries? It would appear that the impersonal sharing of data over electronic networks is not enough to create the kind of mutual trust and respect evident in places like Silicon Valley; for that, face-to-face contact and the reciprocal engagement that comes about as a result of repeated social interaction is necessary. Thus, while the manufacture of commodity-like goods can be outsourced to low labour-cost parts of the world, it is much more difficult to do this with sophisticated technology development.

# Building social capital

Everything that has been said up to this point suggests that modern capitalist economies will generate a continuing demand for social capital. Whether there will be supply of social capital adequate to meet this demand depends on a host of factors, many of them exogenous to the market economy. There are two levels on which the supply question can be answered: that of individual firms and that of the society as a whole, including questions of public policy.

In the case of individual firms, social capital can be built through direct investment in education and training in co-operative skills. There is, of course, a huge business literature on the building of corporate cultures, which are nothing other than attempts to socialize workers in a firm into a series of norms that will improve their willingness to co-operate with one another and build a sense of group identity.[80] Many firms that have moved to flat forms of organization, teams and similar management structures have found that they have had to invest heavily in teaching their blue collar workers to exercise what are in effect white collar managerial skills. Conversion of an auto plant from Fordist to lean production entails a great deal of worker retraining, and many firms have found that the costs of retraining in extremely low social capital areas – for example, in areas of high union militancy and worker-management distrust – are prohibitive.

White collar and particularly professional workers often require less in the way of company-based socialization than their blue collar counterparts, simply because they come to the job having been socialized by their higher and professional educations. Here the issue is frequently not building social capital *per se*, but rather eliminating the barriers that restrict the radius of trust of the various networks within the organization. Some of the barriers typically encountered in a firm include:

- excessive compartmentalization in formal organization
- informal status barriers created within the corporation
- status barriers from larger society
- excessive concern for external boundaries
- networks themselves as possible impediments.

Of these barriers, some (like excessive compartment-alization) are internal to the firm and can be remedied by the firm on its own. Saxenian notes one important difference between Silicon Valley and Route 128 firms was the relatively greater emphasis among the latter on subtle status distinctions that would prevent, for example, a vice president from having lunch with an engineer several echelons down the organization chart. Clearly, many of the social stratifications within a firm mirror the stratifications in the surrounding society; the openness of Californian firms apparently had to do with the fact that most employees were newcomers to the region with little inherited social status. As noted earlier, personal networks can often be counter-productive because they are non-transparent and limited in scope, offering obstacles to the free movement of information and ideas within the organization.

A further problem that firms experience is when their goals in social capital building conflict with those in labour productivity. Many firms over the past decade have sought to build high-trust, flat organizations with empowered workers, while at the same time trying to improve productivity through radical downsizing. Indeed, many firms have pocketed the productivity gains achieved by moving to a flat form of organization and used these gains as an occasion for firing workers. Needless to say, these goals are incompatible. If management is seeking to create a high-trust workplace in which low level workers are empowered to take risks and make decisions independent of supervisors, the last thing it should do is fire half of their colleagues. Managers have to decide whether their productivity gains are going to come through simple reduction of headcount, the better use of technology, or whether they are seeking improved information flow and decision-making on the basis of a self-organizing workplace. Aoki points out that middle managers will have few incentives to discover new ways to delegate authority downwards if they believe that they will lose their livelihoods as a result; he suggests that lifetime employment in large Japanese companies is a necessary counterpart to the proper working of flat organization.[81]

The ability to downsize is an important competitive advantage made necessary by technological change. On the other hand, radical re-engineering including wholesale dismissals has become something of a management fad in the United States, carried out to the point where it cuts into valuable human and social capital and a firm's ability to grow. However, there now appears to be a growing recognition that it is hard to continue to make productivity gains by firing workers, and growth has now reappeared as a topic in management-consulting circles.[82]

Many of the most important trust networks and social

norms will, however, be completely exogenous to an individual firm rooted in the social practices of the surrounding society. The supply of social capital is mediated by a host of institutions nearly as broad as society itself: families, schools, churches, voluntary associations, professional societies, popular culture and the like. Most of these institutions are wholly exogenous to the market economy: some, like schools, are funded by tax dollars as public goods; others, like families or voluntary associations, produce social capital as a by-product of other activities. As James Coleman has pointed out, social capital, like many forms of human capital, is a public good, and therefore subject to systematic under-investment by competitive markets. Firms will have an incentive to invest in firm specific social capital – e.g. socializing workers into their particular corporate culture – but will tend not to invest in non-firm specific social capital because of free rider problems.

We are thus led to the question of generating social capital in the broader society. To understand how this can be done, we need to look more systematically at the question of the sources of social capital.

# Part 3: The Origins of Order

The first two parts of this paper have dealt, respectively, with the low and high ends of the distribution of social capital in post-industrial societies. Social deviance statistics across the OECD suggest that social capital has indeed been disappearing in certain sectors of each society, while the demand and probably the supply have actually increased in other parts. It is therefore difficult to argue, as Robert Putnam does, that social capital has been declining across the board in the United States or any other developed country; what can be argued is that its distribution is changing. The overall demand for social capital remains at both ends of the distribution, so the problem of supply will remain a continuing challenge. It is therefore necessary to look into the origins of social capital.

# Where does social capital come from?

The subject of where the co-operative norms underlying social capital come from is a huge one, a question that in some ways is coextensive with the field of sociology. Economists, of course, have their own highly developed theory of the origins of co-operative norms – game theory. In recent years, game theory has become dominant in many of the social sciences outside of economics. It is my view that while game theory provides some very useful insights into the origin of norms and an even more useful set of conceptual tools for understanding the problem of co-operation, it represents much too narrow a view of how norms are generated and transmitted.

Game theory poses the following problem of co-operation: how do rational but selfish agents manage to arrive at co-operative norms that maximize group welfare, when they are tempted to defect from the co-operative solution and achieve even higher individual payoffs? The classic problem in game theory is the 'prisoner's dilemma', in which two agents fail to achieve a high co-operative payoff because they are more certain of achieving a lower payoff by defecting. While there may not be a rational solution to a one-shot prisoner's dilemma game, Robert Axelrod showed how an iterated game, in which the same players were forced to interact with one another repeatedly, could be solved through a simple 'tit-for-tat' strategy in which each player reciprocated co-operation for co-operation and defection for defection.[83] A learning process ensued in which each player eventually recognized that in the long run, the co-operative strategy produced a higher individual return than the defection strategy, and hence was rationally optimal.

I do not intend to review the intellectual history of game theory for this audience; I do not have the knowledge or the time here to do justice to what has become an enormous branch of economics. I have no doubt that something like Axelrod's iterated tit-for-tat strategy accurately describes the behaviour of economic agents when the other behavioural preconditions of the theory are met – for example, in the financial markets of highly developed economies where individual agents do indeed behave as rational utility-maximizers. It is clear that corporations seek to develop reputations for trustworthiness not out of ethical concerns, but because it benefits them to do so.

There is a large law and economics literature using game

theoretic methods to describe the emergence of spontaneously generated informal norms regulating economic behaviour. Much of this literature originates from the so-called 'Coase theorem' which states that when transaction costs are zero, a change in the formal rules of liability will have no effect on the allocation of resources.[84] Put differently, in a zero-transaction cost world it is not necessary for governments to intervene to regulate polluters or other producers of negative externalities, because the parties who are negatively affected will have a rational incentive to organize and buy off the miscreant. Social regulatory norms, in other words, will simply arise out of self-interested interactions of individual agents and do not have to be mandated through law or formal institutions.

While the zero-transaction cost requirement is almost never met in any real world situation, economists have by now studied quite a number of intriguing cases of self-organization, whereby social norms have been created through a bottom-up process. Sugden describes rules for the sharing of driftwood,[85] and Ellickson gives numerous examples of spontaneous economic rules, including his own detailed field research on the interactions of ranchers and farmers in Shasta County, California.[86] There are many other fascinating examples which bear looking into, including the ways in which trust norms develop among members of the New York Stock Exchange, the ways in which oil companies share excess capacity and how railroads developed a mechanism for sharing boxcars.

On the other hand, game theory is limited as a general explanation for how social norms are generated. The problem goes straight to the heart of the model of human behaviour underlying modern neo-classical economics: namely, that few human beings enter into economic exchange without bringing with them a host of previously existing social norms that strongly influence their willingness and ability to co-operate.[87] Indeed, there is a lengthy debate associated with Durkheim and Polanyi which argues that market exchange itself is dependent on the existence of prior social norms that determine, among other things, that individual agents will seek to buy and sell rather than try to kill one another and steal their property (as Hobbes suggests they would).[88]

Furthermore, there is a growing literature coming out of the natural sciences that suggests that social co-operation is hard-wired into the genetic structure of primates including man, and that emotions like guilt at the betrayal of members of a group have a basis in the human brain. Game theory has in fact been very useful to evolutionary biologists in understanding how biological organisms achieve evolutionarily stable strategies in interacting with fellow organisms and their environments. But from an evolutionary geneticist's point of view, the selfish actor that maximizes its survival chances is not an individual animal, but a single gene or group of genes controlling some aspect of behaviour, whose 'interest' is to make sure copies of itself are transmitted into subsequent generations.[89] Since related animals share genes and transmit them to their offspring, this leads to behaviour that appears to be altruistic from the standpoint of an individual animal: for example, mothers who sacrifice their own well-being to improve their children's life-chances, members of the same herd or troop warning others of approaching danger at cost to themselves etc. Individual human agents, then, do not start with a set of selfish preferences from which they derive altruistic strategies through a maximizing, game-theoretic process. Their selfish preferences are mixed together with altruistic ones from the start. These preferences work at cross purposes and cannot be simultaneously maximized.

As noted in Part 1, there is growing evidence that other social impulses are genetically grounded. Reciprocal altruism may have evolved as a genetic characteristic through a game theoretic process, since reciprocity turns out to be in the individual organism's selfish interest. But individuals do not necessarily arrive at reciprocity through use of their individual reason; their rational self-interest appears to receive a powerful boost from an instinctive drive in that direction. The biologist Robert Trivers actually ran a prisoner's dilemma game in which co-operation between the prisoners was induced by the presence of a hostile third party in the room – a factor that seems to reflect some inherited predisposition to co-operate, and not the calculations of coolly rational agents.[90]

Thus the problem posed by game theory could easily have been stated differently: how, given the fact that there are strong cultural and biological impulses toward co-operative behaviour, does it come about that co-operation often breaks down?

In reviewing the game-theoretic literature, it is remarkable how little empirical evidence there is showing that an actual social norm of some significance to a given society was actually generated in a game-theoretic manner. There are, of course, many *post hoc ergo propter hoc* arguments, which first seek to discern an economically rational reason for the existence of some social norm, and then go on to assert that the norm must have been generated in a game-theoretic manner.

Let us take, for example, the Confucian rules on filial piety and inheritance which, as I have shown elsewhere, have a significant impact on the development of the Chinese economy. It is possible to argue retrospectively that these rules were a rational adaptation to the environmental conditions of traditional Chinese life.[91] That is, sons were seen as an economic resource that would be particularly important as a form of old-age insurance in a society where no public social security existed. The extremely strong bonds of trust within Chinese families, and the corresponding lack of trust between non-kin, is a rational response to a centralized state that did not respect property rights and engaged in highly arbitrary tax policies. There is, of course, a long-standing debate on the degree to which Confucius himself was an original thinker, and the degree to which he merely codified the social rules in existence at the time he wrote, which may themselves have been rational adaptations on the part of individual Chinese.

All of this is interesting, suggestive, and possibly even true. The problem is that we have not one shred of empirical evidence showing that these norms historically evolved from some kind of iterated game, as opposed, say, to arising out of the pure cultural creativity of Confucius himself or his many disciples and followers. Moreover, we know for a fact that the way in which these norms were transmitted to subsequent generations of individuals in China was in a largely arational manner, that is, through a complex process of socialization ranging from mother-infant relations to formal education.

The same may be said for other historically important social norms. The Protestant Reformation, that Weber held so critical for early capitalist development, might be rooted in some sense in the social-political-economic conditions of central European life in the early sixteenth century. It would be difficult, however, to argue that norms like honesty, frugality savings, and the like were the product of spontaneous interactions of rational agents, rather than a moral teaching springing, in some important sense, straight from the intellect of people like Luther, Calvin and Fox.

It is necessary, therefore, to put game theory in proper perspective. It represents one approach to the problem of social co-ordination, but it must be fitted into a much larger taxonomy of sources of norm-generation.

# A taxonomy of norm-generation

TABLE 3.1, overleaf, outlines several broad ways in which co-operative social norms can be generated:

**1. Institutionally constructed norms.** By institutionally constructed, I mean constructed as a result of intentional action on the part of a community as a whole, usually through an institution like the state. Formal institutions like constitutions and legal systems tend over time also to produce informal social norms. Tocqueville's Democracy

**Table 3.1. Sources of Social Capital**

| | |
|---|---|
| **1.** | **institutionally constructed** |
| **a.** | rational |
| **b.** | irrational |
| **2.** | **spontaneously constructed** |
| **a.** | rational – game theoretic |
| **b.** | irrational – common law model/complex adaptive systems |
| **3.** | **exogenously constructed** |
| **a.** | religion |
| **b.** | ideology |
| **c.** | culture and shared historical experience |
| **4.** | **natural** |
| **a.** | kinship |
| **b.** | race and ethnicity |

in America is a study of social norms such as individualism that resulted from the American regime's formal commitment to equality. By and large, the left has tended to believe that human nature and culture are relatively plastic, and that norms can be shaped by deliberate manipulation. Within this category it is useful to distinguish between rational and irrational institutional construction.

**1a. Rational institutional construction.** The most extreme form of rational constructivism was undertaken by communist states such as the Soviet Union and China. Communism was, of course, a bastard child of the Enlightenment, and shared (albeit in a mutant form) the expectation that societies could be founded on rational principles. The Bolsheviks hoped not only to collectivize formal political and economic institutions, but also to create a 'new Soviet Man' who would be shorn of selfish private interests and oriented towards the good of mankind as a whole. New social norms would be created through agitation, propaganda and an educational system designed to legitimate new Soviet values.

The Soviet Union's massive, seventy-year experiment in social constructivism ended, as we all now know, in total failure: the billions of rubles and man-years invested in agitprop and deliberate socialization resulted in a population that was, if anything, more selfish, inward-looking and atomized than it had been in pre-Bolshevik times, while totally failing to eradicate pre-revolutionary religious, ethnic and cultural identities.

In democratic societies, the chief source of institutionally constructed social norms is law. There is an extensive legal literature that deals with the ways in which formal institutions are responsible for fostering informal ones, for better or worse. For example, Douglass North and Robert Thomas argue that the development of formal property rights in England and Holland in the sixteenth century was critical to the creation of modern capitalism and the informal norms supporting it.[92] Conversely, Diego Gambetta argues that the absence of state-enforced property rights is the source of the pervasive culture of distrust in Sicily.[93]

Outside the family, education is the next most important arena for socialization. It produces a blizzard of different norms: it can lead to the spread of new ideologies or systematic ideas, but for the most part

99

produces norms on a smaller scale. One of the most important sources of norms in a post-industrial economy is professional education, where engineers, doctors, lawyers, accountants or architects are all trained not only in their particular field of speciality, but are also socialized to obey certain behavioural norms concerning professional standards.

One specific use of law that plays a particularly important role in the shaping of social norms is public education. The French education system has sought to inculcate a republican sense of citizenship since the Revolution, while the German school system has sought to eradicate racism and nationalism since the end of the Second World War. American public schools were used to transmit American cultural values, particularly in the first decades of the twentieth century when élites saw the need to assimilate large numbers of immigrants.

**1b. Irrational institutional construction.** Marx argued that social norms had been constructed under capitalism to serve the interests of the bourgeoisie. There are several contemporary versions of this view. Feminists have for years argued that female social roles are the result of unjust male domination and patriarchy. Many postmodernists like Foucault broaden this critique and argue that all behaviour is socially constructed, not on the basis of human beings rationally discussing the best forms of community life, but on the basis of power and hierarchy. Social identities and the norms supporting them have no basis in nature or biology, but are entirely the product of one group seeking to impose its hegemony on another.

**2. Spontaneous construction.** Spontaneous construction is another form of social construction. Rather than arising from law and other formal institutions, however, spontaneously constructed norms evolve through the repeated interactions of members of a community and are not the result of deliberate choice. Spontaneous constructivism constitutes one of the most interesting areas of recent research into norm-generation, and like institutional constructivism can be divided into rational and irrational subcategories.

**2a. Rational spontaneous construction.** It is in this category that the existing literature on game theory belongs. As noted above, game theory provides a rich source of insights into the development of co-operative norms; the problem with the existing literature is simply the tendency of many game theorists to believe that game theory is the only source of norms.

**2b. Irrational spontaneous construction.** In an argument similar to those of the game-theoretic rational spontaneous constructivists, Friedrich Hayek and other Austrian economists argued that social norms are the result of a long-term spontaneous evolution.[94] Hayek stressed, however, that this process is not a rational one, and quotes Hume approvingly to the effect that 'the rules of morality ... are not conclusions of our reason'.[95] By taking this position, Hayek sought to debunk the rational constructivism he saw as the core of the socialist project. With the model of English common law in mind, Hayek argued that social norms are not generally legislated through a formal political process, but are rather the result of the repeated interactions of individuals seeking to achieve common aims. He argues that while formal norms (i.e. law) are necessary for modern economies, they are by and large a modern invention and do not account for the vast majority of actual norms that constitute a civilization. Because they evolve spontaneously as a result of the continuing interaction of communities with their environment, such norms are highly adaptive. Political freedom is necessary, in Hayek's view, to protect the complex web of evolved social norms that emerge in an open society.

Hayek's description of social norm-formation anticipated the rise of studies in so-called 'complex adaptive systems' in the natural sciences.[96] Over the past fifteen years, there has been a great deal of interest in the emergence of spontaneous order through the arational interactions of simple agents, a process that is pervasive in biological systems. Flocks of birds and hives of bees exhibit high degrees of order which do not arise out of any centralized form of institutional control; rather, the individual agents making up each community interact on the basis of relatively simple behavioural rules to produce much more complex behaviours. The very origins of life are seen to be the result of this kind of process, where the random combinations of various proteins in a primordial soup suddenly produced higher-order, self-replicating molecules.

Studies in complex adaptive systems have led to formal models and attempts to apply the theory beyond its origins in biology to social and economic systems. A market, for example, can be described as a complex adaptive system in which individual agents collectively achieve Pareto-optimal resource allocation through the pursuit of their own narrow maximizing strategies. Social good is not deliberately sought by anyone, and yet arises spontaneously out of activities on the part of individual agents at a lower level of organization.

**3. Exogenous construction.** By exogenous construction, I mean that the norms originate somewhere other than in the community in which they come to be applied, or else through the interaction of that community with its external environment. Most major religions are imported from outside and at times forcibly imposed on populations; Christianity, Buddhism and Islam all originated in places other than the societies where they received their greatest development.

There has been a longstanding historical argument about the extent to which cultural or religious norms can be truly exogenous. The growth and spread of any religious movement has been linked to pre-existing social and economic conditions, and indeed it would seem likely that conditions need to be ripe in certain ways for religious movements to take root. The Reformation's spread in the early sixteenth century has been attributed to objective conditions in the Church, or to the political needs of various princes and rulers in central Europe. Nonetheless, interpretations like those of Marx that argue that religious and cultural ideas are simply the product of underlying social and economic conditions seldom do justice to the actual historical phenomenon involved. They fail to give due weight to the creative genius of the people who found new religions or cultural systems, and they underplay the degree to which norms shape institutions and economic forces.

**3a. Religion.** Weber pointed to the importance of religion not simply in creating the work ethic, but in promoting trust networks that were conducive to entrepreneurship and economic exchange. Coleman gives the example of diamond merchants in New York City who typically leave bags of precious stones in each others' keeping without receipts or other formal legal instruments; they can do so because they all belong to the same orthodox Jewish sect from Poland and have a variety of communal forms of authority that can be brought to bear on people who break the rules.[97]

On the right, there is a strong tendency to think that social norms come largely if not exclusively from religion. By this view, the principal reason for the changes in social norms is the spread of secular values throughout society. The cure for the problem of deficient norms is therefore more religion.

There is obviously a great deal of truth to this point of view if viewed as a historical proposition. Religion does and will have an important continuing role in modern societies; earlier theories of secularism as the inevitable consequence of modernization are clearly wrong.[98]

On the other hand, many norms in industrialized societies do not come from religion, and in many cases it is difficult to find any simple empirical correlation between religious practice and norm-driven behaviour. For example, it is not clear that there has been a massive decrease in religious belief in the period corresponding to the decline in social capital described by Robert Putnam. (There has, of course, been a massive shift in the relationship of *public* authority and religion in the United States since mid-twentieth century, which is probably what most people think of when they assume there has been a decline in religious practice.) By a variety of measures, religious belief and practice continues to be far stronger and more widespread in the United States than in other industrialized countries; certainly, it would be hard to argue that the small decline in church attendance between the 1950s and the 1990s could account for the massive changes in moral standards that occurred over that period.[99] If norm-driven behaviour were strongly correlated with secularism, then most European countries should be experiencing much higher levels of social breakdown than the United States. As indicated in Part 1, many European countries have levels of family breakdown as high or higher than the United States, but in other measures of social deviance like crime they are much more law-abiding.

**3b. Ideology.** Particularly in the modern world, ideas cross political and cultural borders quite readily, and become the basis for group affiliation. These ideas can be secular and instrumentally rational: political parties, environmental, feminist, labour, terrorist and other groups all act out of a commitment to a common political-ideological agenda. The entire non-governmental sector, that many people identify with civil society *tout court*, tends to be organized around ideological norms.

**3c. Culture and shared historical experience.** While a great deal of culture stems from religion, there are many other sources of cultural norms that do not have the transcendental origin we associate with religion. The Jews and Armenians, for example, are bound by a common religion and ethnicity, but are also shaped by common experiences of persecution that create solidarities of a different sort. Many cultural phenomena can have relatively recent political or economic roots: hence the post-war German central bank's emphasis on a strong Deutschmark and a tough anti-inflationary policy is said to be a direct outcome of the German experience with hyperinflation during the Weimar period.

**4. Norms rooted in Nature.** Despite the changes in family structure described in Part 1, kinship remains the most powerful form of social relationship in contemporary societies. As I indicated in *Trust* (1995), the importance of kinship relative to other kinds of social structures varies considerably from one society to another, but there is no society in which it has completely withered away.

Beyond the family, classical liberalism argues that man in the state of nature is an isolated individual, one who comes together with other human beings in civil society only as a means of satisfying his selfish appetites. While differing in many particulars, Hobbes, Locke and

Rousseau all deny that man is sociable by nature and see duties to others as derivative of rights. Modern liberal politics and modern neo-classical economics both begin from this individualistic premise.[100]

There is considerable evidence from the natural sciences that suggests that sociability is in fact natural not only to man but to many other primate species as well. While this sociability is to a degree rooted in and reinforced by culture, culture itself is not unique to *homo sapiens*, and there is evidence that certain basic tendencies toward sociability are hard-wired into the genetic code. The anthropologist Lionel Tiger has suggested that male bonding is instinctive to human beings as an evolutionary response to the co-operative needs of hunter-gatherer societies.[101] James Q. Wilson has recently summarized a great deal of what is now known about the grounding of moral action in human nature. [102]

Ethnicity and race are to a large extent socially-constructed categories with no firm grounding in biology or nature. The fact that people can be put in a single racial or ethnic category does not necessarily mean that they will share norms or co-operate for common purposes. Yet people believe both categories to be important sources of identity, and therefore they are *de facto*. It would be surprising if there were not some biological basis for group affiliation based on ethnicity and race, and the latter serves as an important basis for economic enterprise.[103]

Obviously, not all moral action is grounded in nature. One of the points made in Part 1 is that biology is less determinative of male than of female behaviour in families, and therefore needs a greater degree of social reinforcement. Indeed, nature produces such profoundly asocial instincts that certain cultural rules, such as those guaranteeing male economic resources to women and children, exist as near-universals.

This list of sources of norms probably does not exhaust the topic, but serves at least to give some idea of the scope and complexity of the problem. Many of these sources are not mutually exclusive: norms grounded in nature can be reinforced by positive law, religion and spontaneously generated social constraints simultaneously. Much of the discussion of the origins of norms is politically loaded: the left has traditionally argued that norms are institutionally grounded, and can be shaped as a result of deliberate policy by states and other institutions. The right, for its part, tends to argue that norms arise from religion, culture or nature, and that these norms are themselves a constraint on the ability of states or institutions to shape human interactions. Needless to say, there is some truth in both points of view; what is important is to understand the full range of sources for norm-generation and to understand the opportunities and limits of each. As it turns out, the choice of source for social norm generation is quite important; institutional means cannot readily substitute for spontaneous or exogenous norm-creation and vice versa.

## Rationality and Family Decline
The discussion of the causes of the decline in Part 1 pointed

to two variables that played a particularly important role: the development of birth control and the shift in relative earnings from men to women. The latter in particular is very much in line with Gary Becker's neo-classical economic interpretation of family life. It treats marriage and fertility as essentially economic behaviours that are influenced by relative prices: hence the mother's potential earnings affects her desire for children, etc.[104] This suggests that game-theoretic and other rational actor approaches may be appropriate for studying the problem of norm shift in this important case.

The problem with using a rational actor approach to family norms is not that it takes economic factors too seriously, but that it does not develop an empirical theory of preferences based either on biology or culture. In all animal species, the parent-child relationship involves a large, one-way transfer of time, energy, resources and emotional involvement. Becker and other economists can explain family behaviour only by including altruism toward children as part of the parents' utility function, or by seeing children as investments that will pay direct (rather than emotional) benefits. It is questionable whether it makes sense to describe altruism as a form of utility; if economics is not at base the science of individual selfishness, it is hard to see what it teaches us about human behaviour. Indeed, a commonsense reaction to Becker is that the family is one area of social life clearly not subject to economic rationality, and where love and emotion necessarily override individual self-interest.

The social problem of the family, then, results from the fact that the interests of children are *not* optimized by parents rationally pursuing their individual self-interests. The family has been a successful institution over the ages only because human beings are not simply the rational utility-maximizers postulated by neo-classical economics, but are driven by their natures to make large non-economic sacrifices on behalf of their children.

The problem that arises in post-industrial societies concerns gender differences with regard to parental altruism. It is evident that the altruistic preference for children appears to be much stronger on the part of women than men. While the latter have genetically based preferences for their own offspring, they also have preferences for fathering further children, often by different mothers, that will be rival claimants to their resources. In other words, men when compared to women have preferences that are in part consistently biased against the interests of their children. If left free to maximize their interests as rational agents, it is not at all clear that they will be induced to make those one-way sacrifices necessary for the rearing and education of their children. The fact that so many men have in recent years voluntarily taken steps that injure the life-chances of their children when released from social obligations to stay with their original families indicates that this is in fact the case.

To an economist, economic goods are fungible: if those resources necessary to provide for a mother and her dependent children are not forthcoming from biological fathers in the context of traditional nuclear families, then they can come equally well from the mother's independent income or from the state. Unfortunately, there is a good deal of evidence that indicates that this isn't so. As David Popenoe has documented at great length, fathers play an extremely important role in raising of both sons and daughters, and they are much more likely to play that role well if they are the biological father of the child in question.[105] Hence it may be the case that men and women, interacting in a game-theoretic manner as rational maximizing agents, are developing new co-operative social norms for family life and the raising of children. But while these new norms of fatherlessness and male irresponsibility may serve to maximize the interests of the mothers and fathers, it is by no means clear that they are in the interests of children. A game-theoretic interaction might therefore lead to an overall result that is far from socially optimal.

Hayek might argue that the process of spontaneous norm-generation is still going on, and that post-industrial societies may yet generate new norms that come closer to a social optimum given contemporary economic conditions. A neo-Darwinian might assert that if in fact existing norms were suboptimal for the life-chances of future generations, then those parents exhibiting this behaviour will have fewer and weaker children, ultimately reproducing themselves less well than other parents with different preferences. Neither of these propositions is, needless to say, a comforting thought from the standpoint of short-term social policy.

## Public policy implications

The taxonomy above suggests that social capital is typically created outside of the public sector, either through a process of spontaneous generation, or else through what was labelled 'exogenous' generation – as the by-product of religion, culture or other forms of shared historical experience. Social capital is created daily in a host of situations, from two individuals who become friends and come to share a norm of reciprocity, to a firm that socializes workers, to a common 'corporate culture' as described in Part 2 and a political movement started by a group of activists.

Social capital is in some respects a public good: its benefits are often widely dispersed and therefore not readily appropriable by the agent responsible for creating it. This suggests that there will be limits to the degree to which market actors will have an incentive to supply social capital. To the extent it is a public good, it must be supplied either by a government agency, or by a non-governmental actor outside of the market economy such as a church or a voluntary association.

Public agencies have created social capital in a variety of ways. One of the most basic functions of a state (to which any neo-classical economist would assent), is the protection of property rights through a transparent rule of law. In situations where states fail to perform this function, e.g. historically in southern Italy or today in Russia or the Ukraine, private organizations enter the protection business and private trust plummets.

In addition, public agencies can foster more specific kinds of social capital. Military organizations, for example, deliberately foster group solidarity through an intensive process of socialization, because unit cohesion is critical to military effectiveness.[106] Agricultural extension officers were frequently responsible for creating webs of community solidarity in the rural areas in which they operated during the first part of the twentieth century. And state school systems from the United States to France to Japan, in addition to imparting conventional forms of human capital, have socialized children to common cultural rules.

On the other hand, states are capable of depleting social capital when they seek to take over functions better left to civil society. The classic case of this was France, where a series of ambitious monarchs centralized political authority in Paris and created a society where, in Tocqueville's phrase, there were not ten Frenchmen who could come together for a common purpose. The negative influence of welfare programs like AFDC on social capital in poor families has already been discussed in Part I. In recent years, the United States has seen the proliferation of multicultural education curricula which are designed to raise the self-esteem of different minority groups by emphasizing the virtues of their unique histories and cultures. Such programs, while understandable, deplete social capital by building unnecessary walls between different racial and ethnic groups. The first rule for public policy, then, is to do no harm. That is, states ought to resolutely produce those public goods which only they can provide, like the protection of rights, education, defence and the like. At the same time, they ought to leave to civil society those functions better performed by smaller, less centralized and bureaucratic institutions.

In terms of positive actions, governments need to begin by performing consistently and well those functions for which they are uniquely suited. In the current anti-statist era, it is sometimes forgotten that the pursuit of neo-classical economic orthodoxy requires that governments perform certain key functions, particularly the transparent and impersonal protection of property rights and the provision of public goods like security and public education. Governments contribute to private distrust and deplete the stock of social capital not only when they take over functions properly played by civil society, but also when they fail to provide public goods. The high levels of social distrust, crime and public corruption in societies like southern Italy, China and Russia can be traced in large measure to states which failed to protect property rights, and consequently encouraged the proliferation of private agents seeking to provide protection – an economists' way of describing mafia-like organizations.

There is a whole cluster of public policy issues arising from the Great Disruption, particularly in the United States where its consequences for social capital have been most severe. The analysis presented in Part 1 suggests that broad shifts in technology and labour markets have been at the root of changing gender and family norms. The case of Japan shows that it is, at the limit, possible to reverse family decline through public policy. If Western countries were to re-introduce discriminatory labour laws that kept women out of labour markets and did not permit them to earn comparable wages to men, then the resulting dependence of women on male incomes would probably help to restore traditional two-parent families.

Needless to say, this is not a real policy option for anyone. Indeed, it is hard to see how Japan and other industrialized Asian countries are going to be able to avoid significantly higher rates of female labour force participation and greater wage equality given the extreme labour shortages they are going to face in the first half of the twenty-first century.

Assuming that no one is prepared as a moral or practical matter to suggest turning back the clock, a number of other policy recommendations suggest themselves.

One general conclusion is that public policies need to be more gender-specific in their targeting and design. Needless to say, this runs against the grain of many recent changes in public policy, which have sought to uproot and eliminate all gender-specific laws. Gender differentiation has been treated as if it were something akin to racial discrimination; institutions open to boys and not girls, or policies with different effects on men and women, have been challenged as unconstitutional.

This trend obviously reflects the fact that there has been a great deal of gender discrimination in the past. On the other hand, gender is very different from race: while the biological evidence for serious and consistent differences between human races is small to non-existent, the evidence for serious gender differences is legion. Men and women are different in their underlying psychological make-up; they face different incentives with regard to family life and child-rearing; and they pose different risks to society in terms of aggression and asocial behaviour. Public policies that seek to be gender-blind in the way they are supposed to be colour-blind are therefore bound to have unanticipated consequences.

One way to become more gender-specific is simply in the way we describe the problem. For example, while it may have been the movement of women into the paid labour force that lies at the heart of the Great Disruption, the real behavioural problems have all been on the side of men. To talk neutrally about family breakdown ignores the fact that men and women are not equally complicit in creating the social problem. Women, even working women with high-powered careers, still tend to invest more of their time in child-rearing than men. The real problem is men, who feel today that they have been released from the obligation to stay with their wives and particularly with the children they father. There is no deficit of mothers and motherhood; there is, however, a serious deficit of fathers and fatherhood. Policies therefore need to be very much aimed at changing male behaviour and incentives through new cultural values or different forms of socialization. I will illustrate this principle with regard to two areas of public policy: welfare and worker retraining.

**1. Welfare reform targeted at fathers rather than mothers.** In 1996 the United States Congress finally passed a major welfare reform bill that ended the federal entitlement to unlimited welfare benefits, and closed down the Depression-era Aid to Families with Dependent Children (AFDC) program. One of the critical justifications for this reform cited by its backers was the negative effects of AFDC on family stability among the poor.

The most significant critique of the 1996 welfare reform bill was made by James Q. Wilson in a speech to the Manhattan Institute a year earlier in 1995. Along the lines of the analysis above, Wilson argued that the real behavioural problem encouraged by the current welfare system is not single mothers on welfare who don't want to work, but rather the fathers of their children who take no responsibility for their offspring once they are born. However the current welfare bill changes incentives for poor families, they will operate entirely on the mother's side. There is an unstated hope that by removing incentives for women to become single parents, the men's behaviour will also change – presumably as a result of the women denying sex to the men unless they return the traditional exchange of fertility for stability and resources. It is extremely dubious that anything like this will actually occur. Moreover, from the standpoint of young children, it is not clear it is desirable for the mothers to be working.

Far more important is to restore fatherhood, something that requires a positive act of re-socialization so that the men recover a sense of responsibility for the children they produce. To accomplish this requires, in turn, a solution to the problem that the fathers are unemployable and therefore have no resources to offer the mothers as their part of the bargain. It is not clear to me that whatever little money will be spent on job training and job creation as mothers move from welfare to work would not be better spent on providing incentives to the fathers and making them employable.

**2. Worker training.** The disappearance of high wage, low skill jobs in sectors like automobiles, steel, meatpacking and the like is a universal problem for all industrialized countries. This job loss accounts for the continuing high rates of unemployment in Europe and for the falling real working-class wages in the United States. It is a problem that is bound to become more severe as the Third World develops and more low-skill workers enter the global labour market. It is, as the account of the Great Disruption above indicates, also one of the sources of family breakdown and the various pathologies accompanying the shift in gender roles.

Those low-skill workers most severely affected are males rather than females. I pointed out, in Part 1, that male median incomes, measured in constant dollars, peaked in the United States around 1972 or 1973, and have been decreasing slightly ever since, while male labour force participation has been declining. That is, any gains in household income realized since that time have come as a result of women entering the work force or receiving higher incomes. The talk of 'angry white males' in American politics reflects this economic fact. Given the steady gains achieved by women, it would seem reasonable to target job training programs specifically at this group.

A number of European countries have undertaken active labour market policies to help workers make the transition from dead-end jobs into new areas of employment, the most famous of which is probably the German apprenticeship program. This has in recent years run into problems because it costs too much for the training it provides, and is also not promoting the right set of skills for an information-age economy. By contrast, the German higher education system is not producing nearly enough highly-trained professionals to meet requirements at the upper end of the labour market.

The situation in the United States is the complete opposite: American higher education continues to be first class, both in terms of quality and quantities of students educated, but the record on worker training is poor. There are currently some forty federal and countless state worker retraining programs, the first of which consume some $25 billion of the federal budget every year, and as a group they are generally recognized to be abysmal failures.[107] The American system of vocational education is very weak compared to that of central Europe; for the most part, low-skill workers are simply left to fend for themselves in acquiring the skills needed to remain employed.

Adding urgency to the worker retraining issue is the shifting age composition of all OECD countries. Owing to steady drops in fertility, almost all OECD countries will be losing population at a dramatic rate by the middle of the twenty-first century. Using the low-growth fertility assumptions of the United Nations Population Office's estimates for global population, populations in countries like Germany, Italy and Japan will decline at a rate of about 1 per cent per year by the middle of the next century. Even more worrying is the fact that the median age will drift steadily upward, moving to fifty-eight years for Italy by 2050, fifty-three years for Germany and fifty-four years for Japan. Most economists are aware of the huge social security liability problem this creates. Given advances in the health of the elderly population, it would seem inevitable that working careers are going to extend and retirement ages will be pushed back. If people routinely retire at seventy-five or eighty rather than sixty-five, it would seem all the more mandatory that training and education are ongoing processes rather than something that is accomplished before the age of twenty-five. The likelihood that job skills are still going to be valuable fifty or sixty years after they are acquired seems, to say the least, implausible.

# Social capital and post-industrial society

I began Part I by noting that many critics of the Enlightenment argued that a society founded solely on the principles of reason, without help from religion, tradition and culture, would ultimately become self-undermining. Though they did not use the term 'social capital', they were concerned whether a political system that limited the powers of the state and depended heavily on institutions to regulate the pursuit of self-interest would generate within itself sufficient sources of social order to avoid slipping into anarchy.

Despite the collapse of Communism and the evident failure of virtually all serious competitors to the liberal-democratic Enlightenment order, the verdict is still not in. As the industrial period gives way to the post-industrial era, and as information and services become the chief sources of new wealth in the economy, informal social norms play a renewed role in innovation and production. The collapse of Taylorite scientific management signals the limits of organization founded solely on rule-based bureaucratic rationalism; its replacement by flat or networked forms of management and self-organization signal the continuing requirement for informal norm-based co-ordination. And to some extent, the increasing demand for such norm-based organization is calling forth a corresponding supply. Robert Putnam is simply wrong to assert an across-the-board decline in American social capital: there are some sectors of American society that probably have higher levels of social capital than in previous historical periods.

On the other hand, economic change has made the Great Disruption possible, which in turn has undermined certain critical co-operative norms related to the family and spawned a host of related social pathologies. It is not clear that we are moving spontaneously toward the creation of a new set of norms regarding, for example, gender relations, that will serve as a socially-optimal substitute with regard to such functions as the socialization of children. Under these circumstances, the state has intervened to mitigate the consequences of these shifting norms, usually with less than optimal results and at increasingly great economic cost. The current crisis of the welfare state is this: even if it were affordable, it is not clear that the state can adequately perform the socialization functions traditionally played by other, smaller-scale social groups and without hastening the demise of those very groups.

If the state is finally incapable of rebuilding social capital, the question is whether it will come from other sources. My earlier taxonomy of norm-generation suggests that apart from rational institutional sources, norms can be generated spontaneously through the repeated interactions of individual agents, or exogenously through the introduction of a new set of moral norms. Hayek suggests that informal social norms are constantly in the process of evolution, and that over time free individuals, if left to their own devices, will arrive at ones suitable to their circumstances. Stated in this fashion, Hayek's assertion is unfalsifiable; any problematic set of norms is necessarily in the process of evolving to something different and potentially better. The question is how long this evolution will take, what mechanisms might intervene to speed up the process and how much damage will be done in the meantime.

We can draw some comfort by looking at other historical periods, and noting that societies have been able to regenerate social capital in the past. Historical data on social trends are necessarily sketchy, but it is clear that the levels of social deviance evident in the developed world today are not historically unprecedented. The Industrial Revolution in England had, by the early nineteenth century, produced a host of social pathologies including high levels of murder and robbery, family breakdown, abandonment of children, alcoholism and the like.[108] A number of sources suggest that deviance rates rose steadily through the middle of the nineteenth century, and thereafter began a long, slow decline.

The causes of that decline are complex. Religion clearly played a role: the Wesleyan movement in the first half of the century had, as E. P. Thompson has shown, had a profound influence on the British working class, and was able to arrest the spread of social decay.[109] Victorian morality, which has

**Figure 3.1: Homicide rate, US, 1900–94**

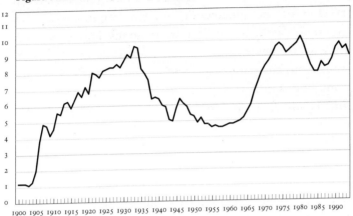

come in for extraordinary criticism in the late twentieth century, was in many respects understood as a deliberate effort to counteract the breakdown in norms that had occurred earlier in the century.

Something similar has also happened in the United States. If we look, for example, at homicide data and extend it back far enough, it becomes evident that current murder rates are not unprecedented. As FIGURE 3.1, above, indicates, as recently as the 1930s Americans were murdering each other at levels similar to today. As in Britain, the United States saw dramatic increases in crime rates as it went through its first phase of industrialization, followed by a gradual fall at the end of the nineteenth century.[110] Civil society has been disrupted by the transition from an agricultural to an industrial society, but many new institutions that would come to dominate the American social order by the middle of the twentieth century – the symphony halls, universities

123

and voluntary associations – were creations of the decades at the end of the nineteenth and the beginning of the twentieth centuries. American religious life, as is well known, has never been on a one-way descent towards secularism, but rather has experienced periodic upsurges from the Great Awakenings of the eighteenth and nineteenth centuries to the Pentecostal revival in the twentieth. All of this suggests that the Great Disruption will call forth countervailing efforts to remoralize and restore the social norms broken by economic change.

If, as I mentioned in Part 1, the field of sociology is seen as one long commentary on the transition from *Gemeinschaft* to *Gesellschaft*, then it is clear that this transition has entered a new phase with the transition to a post-industrial society in which work has been feminized and gender relations put on a new basis. The great classic figures of social theory – Marx, Tönnies, Weber, Durkheim and Simmel – need to be written anew to take account of what is easily as momentous a shift as the one they experienced during their own lives.

# Appendix:
# A more precise measure of social capital

Coming up with a more adequate measure of social capital involves the inclusion of several other variables excluded from Putnam's measures. Putnam is essentially counting groups in civil society, using a number $n$ to track membership in sports clubs, bowling leagues, literary societies, political clubs and the like as it varies over time and across different geographical regions. As noted in Part 1, the absence of families from the universe of $n$'s is one starting limitation in Putnam's use of this measure. In any given society, there are in fact a large number of $n$'s: $n_{1 \cdots t}$. The variable $t$ itself constitutes a separate of measure of civil society; unfortunately, limitations in the data prohibit our knowledge what $t$ is for a given society, or how many missing or undercounted data elements there are between $n_1$ and $n_t$. N and $t$ may be inversely correlated (that is, the larger the average size of groups, the fewer there are); on the other hand, because individuals can hold overlapping memberships in multiple groups, they need not be. The first measure for the total social capital (SC) in a society is the sum of the membership of all groups and can be expressed as:

$$SC = \Sigma n_{1 \cdots t}$$

Both $n$ and $t$ are important measures of civil society. A small value for $n$ may limit the kinds of ends a group can achieve; families, for example, are good at socializing children and running family restaurants, but are not very good at exerting political influence or at manufacturing semiconductors.

It is clear that each of these $n_{1 \cdots t}$ groups is characterized by a different level of internal cohesion and therefore collective action. As noted in Part 1, bowling leagues are not capable of storming beaches or lobbying Congress, so some qualitative coefficient must be added to provide some measure of cohesion. Let us call this coefficient $c$. Unfortunately, there is no accepted method for measuring the internal cohesiveness of groups; each one of the $c$ coefficients would have to be determined subjectively by an outside observer who would note the types of activities the group could undertake and their difficulty, its cohesion under stressful circumstances and other such factors. Despite the subjective nature of its derivation, it is clear that $c$ varies across groups and is a critical qualitative measure of social capital. Hence a society's total stock of social capital would be expressed as:

$$SC = \Sigma(cn)_{1 \cdots t}$$

In addition to the quantity of groups and their cohesiveness, there is a third factor to consider – the so-called 'radius of trust', that is, the proportion of members of the group sharing tight bonds of trust and able to interact with each other on the basis of shared norms and values. The radius of trust can be thought of as a type of positive externality (which I will therefore designate as $r_p$) because it is a benefit that accrues to the group independent of the collective action the group formally seeks to achieve. For example, a sect that encourages its members to be honest and reliable will foster better business relationships when they deal with each other economically, in addition to the sect's religious objectives.

For many groups, the radius of trust would extend to the whole group; this is true of most families, for example. The $r_p$ coefficient in this case is 1, and the total amount of social capital in the society would therefore be expressed as

$$SC = \sum(r_p cn)_{1 \cdots t}$$

Certain groups, particularly larger ones, are characterized by internal hierarchy, a division of labour, status and functional distinctions etc. While the group may be united around some common interest or passion, the degree to which individual members are capable of collective action on the basis of mutual trust depends on their relative position within the organization. Putnam rightly distinguishes between what he calls a 'membership organization' like the American Association of Retired People (AARP), which, at more than 33 million members, is second only to the Catholic Church in size. Such a group has a very large $n$ value, but most of its members simply contribute yearly dues, receive a newsletter and would have little reason for co-operating with one another on any issue not related to pensions or health benefits. For such an organization, the $r_p$ coefficient may be very small, limited to, for example, those people who work full time in its national headquarters (though even there, there are presumably many employees who are simply wage-earners and not part of the trust network).

On the other hand, it is possible for a group to have an $r_p$ coefficient larger than 1. To take the earlier example of the religious sect that encourages honesty and reliability, if these traits are demanded of its members in their dealings not just with other members of the sect but generally in their dealings with other people, then there will be a positive spillover effect into the larger society. Again, Weber argued in effect that sectarian Puritans had an $r_p$ value greater than 1.

The final factor affecting a society's supply of social capital concerns not the internal cohesiveness of groups, but rather the way in which they relate to outsiders. Strong moral bonds within a group in some cases may actually serve to *decrease* the degree to which members of that group are able to trust outsiders and work effectively with them. A highly disciplined, well-organized group sharing strong common values may be capable of highly co-ordinated collective action, and yet may nonetheless be a social liability. In *Trust*, I noted that strongly familistic societies like China and central-southern Italy were characterized by an absence of a broader, generalized social trust outside the family. At best, this prevents the group from receiving beneficial influences from the outside environment; at worst, it may actively breed distrust, intolerance, or even hatred for and violence toward outsiders. Certain groups may be actively harmful to other parts of society – criminal organizations like the Mafia or the Crips and Bloods come to mind. A society made up of Ku Klux Klan, the Nation of Islam, the Michigan Militia and various self-regarding ethnic and racial organizations may score very high in terms of the last three of the four variables in the last equation, and each group may have an $r_p$ of 1, yet overall it would be hard to say that such a society had a large stock of social capital.

Group affiliation can therefore produce a negative externality which we can think of as the radius of distrust, or $r_n$. The larger the $r_n$ value, the greater the liability that group represents to the surrounding society; hence the measure for a single group's social capital, $r_p c \, n$, needs to be multiplied by the reciprocal of $r_n$. (All $r_n$ values, we assume, must be 1 or greater.) The final value for a society's total stock of social capital would then be:

$$SC = \Sigma((1/r_n)\ r_p cn)_{1\cdots t}$$

To some extent, we could expect that $c$ and $r_n$ might be positively correlated with one another. That is, internal cohesiveness is often based on strongly shared norms and values within a group: the Marines and the Mormon Church are both examples. But the very strength of those internal bonds creates something of a gulf between members of the group and those on the outside. Latitudinarian organizations like most contemporary mainline Protestant denominations in the United States, by contrast, easily coexist with other groups in the society, and yet are capable of a much lower level of collective action. Ideally, one would like to maximize the $c$ and minimize the $r_n$ values: such would be the case, for example, in a professional organization that socializes its members into the values of its particular profession, while at the same time not breeding distrust of other professions or closed to influences from them.

# Notes

## Part 1

1   These are the broad themes of *Trust: The Social Virtues and the Creation of Prosperity*, Free Press, New York, 1995.

2   Jane Jacobs, *The Death and Life of Great American Cities*, Vintage Books, New York, 1961, p. 138.

3   Glen Loury, et.al. *Ethnic Enterprise in America*, University of California Press, Berkeley, 1972.

4   James S. Coleman, 'Social Capital in the Creation of Human Capital', *American Journal of Sociology*, Supplement 94, 1988, S95–S120; 'The Creation of Destruction of Social Capital: Implications for the Law', *Journal of Law, Ethics, and Public Policy* 3, 1988, pp. 375–404; Robert D. Putnam, *Making Democracy Work : Civic Traditions in Modern Italy*, Princeton University Press, Princeton, 1993; 'Bowling Alone: America's Declining Social Capital', *Journal of Democracy* 6, 1995, pp. 65–78.

5   Diego Gambetta, *The Sicilian Mafia: The business of private protection*, Harvard University Press, Cambridge, 1993, p. 35.

6   See, for example, Edward C. Banfield, *The Moral Basis of a Backward Society*, Free Press, Glencoe, 1958, and Robert D. Putnam, *Making Democracy Work: Civic Traditions in Modern Italy*, Princeton University Press, Princeton, 1993.

7   According to Weber, 'The great achievement of ethical religions, above all of the ethical and asceticist sects of Protestantism, was to shatter the fetters of the sib.' *The Religion of China*, Free Press, New York, 1951, p. 237.

8   See, for example, John Gray, *Enlightenment's Wake: Politics and Culture at the Close of the Modern Age*, Routledge, London, 1995.

9   Robert D. Putnam, *Making Democracy Work*, Princeton University Press, Princeton, 1993 and 'Bowling Alone: America's Declining Social Capital', *Journal of Democracy* 6, 1995.

10  Everett C. Ladd, 'The Data Just Don't Show Erosion of America's "Social Capital"', *Public Perspective*, 1996: pp. 4–22; 'The Myth of Moral Decline', *The Responsive Community* 52, Winter 1993; Michael Schudson, 'What If Civic Life Didn't Die?' *American Prospect*, 1996, pp. 17–20; John Clark, 'Shifting Engagements: Lessons from the "Bowling Alone" Debate', *Hudson Briefing Papers* no. 196, October 1996.

11  David Popenoe, *Disturbing the Nest: Family Change and Decline in Modern Societies*, Aldine de Gruyter, New York, 1988, p. 34.

12  This argument is made, for example, in Ladd, 'The Myth of Moral Decline', *The Responsive Community* 52, Winter 1993.

13  Sara McLanahan and Lynne Casper, 'Growing Diversity and Inequality in the American Family', in Reynolds Farley, ed., *State of The Union: America in the 1990s. Volume Two: Social Trends*, Russell Sage Foundation, New York, 1995.

14  On this point, see Seymour Martin Lipset, *American Exceptionalism: A double-edged sword*, W. W. Norton, New York, 1994.

15  William J. Goode, *World Change in Divorce Patterns*, Yale University Press, New Haven, 1993, p. 54.

16  US Bureau of Census, *Statistical Abstract of the United States*, US Government Printing Office, Washington, 1996.

17  See for example McLanahan and Casper in Reynolds Farley, ed., *State of The Union: America in the 1990s. Volume Two: Social Trends*, Russell Sage Foundation, New York, 1995, p. 11.

18  Ibid. p. 77.

19  Daniel Patrick Moynihan, *The Negro Family: A Case for National Action*, Office of Planning and Research, US Dept, of Labor, Washington, March 1965.

20  Sara McLanahan and Gary Sandefur, *Growing Up with a Single Parent: What Hurts, What Helps*, Harvard University Press, Cambridge, 1994, p. 2.

21  David Popenoe, *Life Without Father: Compelling New Evidence that Fatherhood and Marriage Are Indispensable for the Good of Children and Society*, Free Press, New York, 1996, p. 86.

22  On this point, see Derek Bok, *The State of the Nation*, Harvard University Press, Cambridge, 1997, p. 220; James Q. Wilson, 'Criminal Justice in England and America', *The Public Interest* no. 126, Winter 1997, pp. 3-14.

23  See Clifford Geertz, *The Interpretation of Cultures*, Basic Books, New York, 1973, p. 77.

24  This view of the human mind as a *tabula rasa* goes back at least to Locke. For a critique of Skinner, see Lionel Tiger, *The Manufacture of Evil: Ethics, Evolution, and the Industrial System*, Marion Boyars, New York, 1987, pp. 19-21.

25  For an overview, see Robert Wright, *The Moral Animal: Why We Are the Way We Are: The New Science of Evolutionary Psychology*, Vintage Books, New York, 1994.

26  Already there are highly suggestive studies linking behavioural regularities to particular, highly specific parts of the brain, as well as studies in molecular biology linking individual genes or gene segments to inherited traits like breast cancer or obesity. Given the rapidity of progress in these areas, we can only expect more empirical evidence to appear in coming years explicating the biological origins of a good deal of what we have assumed to be social behaviour.

27  Richard Dawkins, *The Selfish Gene*, Oxford University Press, New York 1989.

28  Martin Daly and Margo Wilson, *Homicide*, Aldine de Gruyter, New York, 1968, pp. 17-24.

29  On this point, see Richard Dawkins, *The Selfish Gene*, Oxford University Press, New York 1989; Robert Wright, *The Moral Animal: Why We Are the Way We Are: The New Science of Evolutionary Psychology*, Vintage Books, New York, 1994.

30  Lionel Tiger, *Men in Groups*, Random House, New York, 1969.

31  On this point, see Martin Daly and S. J. Waghorst, 'Male Sexual Jealousy', *Ethology and Sociobiology* 3, 1982, pp. 11-27.

32  For example, Robert Wright points out that the tendency for males to be more promiscuous than females is not only true in virtually all human cultures, it is also true

across primate species and indeed with two or three exceptions, across all vertebrate species. Robert Wright, *The Moral Animal: Why We Are the Way We Are: The New Science of Evolutionary Psychology*, Vintage Books, New York, 1994.

33  Lionel Tiger and Robin Fox, *The Imperial Animal*, Holt, Rinehart, and Winston, New York, 1971.

34  This Darwinian perspective explains why there are so many male polygamists (either simultaneous or serial) across different human cultures and so few female ones, and why conversely there tend to be more unattached low-status males than low-status females. Since the kinship relationship is an exchange of fertility for economic resources, it follows that those males with greater resources and higher status will be able to support a larger number of partners, leaving some males without partners. A wealthy or high-status female, by contrast, would not need the economic resources of multiple partners, nor would multiple partners do much to increase her rate of fertility.

35  Martin Daly and Margo Wilson, *Homicide*, Aldine de Gruyter, New York, 1968, p. 83.

36  Ibid. pp. 86–87; also M. Daly and M. Wilson, 'Children as Homicide Victims', in R. Gelles and J. U. Lancaster, eds., *Child Abuse and Neglect: Biosocial Dimensions*, Aldine de Gruyter, New York, 1987.

37  On this point, see James Q. Wilson and Richard J. Herrnstein, *Crime and Human Nature*, Simon and Schuster, New York, 1985, pp. 104-147.

38  Daniel Patrick Moynihan, *The Negro Family: A Case for National Action*, Office of Planning and Research, US Dept, of Labor, Washington, March 1965.

39  Elaine Ciulla Kamark and William A. Galston, *Putting Children First: A Progressive Family Policy for the 1990s*, Progressive Policy Institute, Washington, 1990, pp. 14-15.

40  James Q. Wilson and Richard J. Herrnstein, *Crime and Human Nature*, Simon and Schuster, New York, 1985, pp. 213-285.

41  This point was made in Coleman (1988): see also Sara McLanahan and Gary Sandefur, *Growing Up with a Single Parent: What Hurts, What Helps*, Harvard University Press, Cambridge, 1994, pp. 5-6.

42  James S. Coleman, *Equality of Educational Opportunity*, US Dept. of HEW, Washington, 1966.

43  A summary of some of the evidence for this is presented in McLanahan and Sandefur, *Growing Up with a Single Parent: What Hurts, What Helps*, Harvard University Press, Cambridge, 1994, pp. 33-35.

44  This argument has been made most recently by Bok, *The State of the Nation*, Harvard University Press, Cambridge, 1997; see also Heidenheimer (198?).

45  David Popenoe surveys the relationship between the Swedish welfare state and family breakdown there in *Life Without Father: Compelling New Evidence that Fatherhood and Marriage Are Indispensable for the Good of Children and Society*, Free Press, New York, 1988, p. 156.

46  Elizabeth Herzog and Cecilia E. Sudia, 'Children in Fatherless Families', in B. Caldwell and H. H. Ricciuti, eds., *Review of Child Development Research*, vol. 3, University of Chicago Press, Chicago, 1973.

47  See the evidence summarized in McLanahan and Sandefur, *Growing Up with a Single*

*Parent: What Hurts, What Helps*, Harvard University Press, Cambridge, 1994, pp. 89–94.

48  This argument was made originally in Charles Murray, *Losing Ground*, Basic Books, New York, 1984. It had actually been made earlier by Gary Becker in his original edition of *Treatise on the Family*, Harvard University Press, Cambridge.

49  The disqualification of married women was actually ended in many states during the 1980s.

50  In a survey of the existing empirical studies of the relationship between welfare and illegitimacy in the United States, Charles Murray himself notes that the relationship is weak for the period after the mid-1970s when average benefit levels in real terms began to decrease, and weaker for blacks than for whites. See Charles Murray, 'Welfare and the Family: The US Experience', *Journal of Labor Economics* 11, vol. 1, part. 2, January 1993,: S224-262.

51  See William A. Galston, 'Beyond the Murphy Brown Debate: Ideas for Family Policy', Speech to the Institute for American Values, Family Policy Symposium, New York City, 1993.

52  For a beautiful evocation of changing norms in one American city, see Alan Ehrenhalt, *The Lost City: Discovering the Forgotten Virtues of Community in the Chicago of the 1950s*, Basic Books, New York, 1995.

53  See Ronald Inglehart, *Modernization and Postmodernization: Cultural, Economic, and Political Change in 42 Societies*, Princeton University Press, Princeton, 1997; Daniel Yankelovich, 'How Changes in the Economy are Reshaping American Values' in Henry Aaron et. al., *Values and Public Policy*, Brookings Institution, Washington, 1994, pp. 18ff.

54  See George Akerlof, Janet Yellen, and Michael L. Katz, 'An Analysis of Out-of-Wedlock Childbearing in the United States', *Quarterly Journal of Economics* 111, no. 2, May 1996, pp. 277-317.

55  On this point, see Gary S. Becker, *A Treatise on the Family*. (enlarged edn.) Harvard University Press, Cambridge, 1991, pp. 141-144.

56  I am grateful to Lionel Tiger for pointing this out.

57  US Dept. of Health and Human Services, *Report to Congress on Out-of-Wedlock Childbearing*, USGPO, Hyattsville, 1995, p. 72.

58  Gary S. Becker, *A Treatise on the Family*. (enlarged edn.) Harvard University Press, Cambridge, 1991, pp. 347-361.

59  See for example Fareed Zakaria, A Conversation with Lee Kuan Yew, *Foreign Affairs* 73 (No. 2, March-April 1994): 109-127.

## Part 2

60  Joseph A. Schumpeter, *Capitalism, Socialism and Democracy*, Harper Brothers, New York, 1950.

61  Daniel Bell, *The Cultural Contradictions of Capitalism*, Basic Books, New York, 1976; see also John K. Galbraith, *The Affluent Society*, Houghton Mifflin Co., Boston, 1958.

62  See, for example, Michael J. Sandel, *Democracy's Discontent: America in Search of a Public*

*Philosophy*, Harvard University Press, Cambridge, 1996.

63 See for example Gernot Grabher, *The Embedded Firm: On the Socioeconomics of Industrial Networks* Routledge, London, 1993; Nitin Nohria and Robert Eccles, eds., *Networks and Organizations: Structure, Form, and Action*, Harvard Business School Press, Boston, 1992; Walter W. Powell, 'Neither Market Nor Hierarchy: Network Forms of Organization', *Research in Organizational Behavior* 12, 1990, pp. 295-336; John L. Casti, David Batten, et. al., *Networks in Action: Communications, Economies and Human Knowledge*, Springer-Verlag, Berlin, 1995; Michael Best, *The New Competition: Institutions of Industrial Restructuring*, Harvard University Press, Cambridge, 1990.

64 Thomas W. Malone and Joanne Yates, 'Electronic Markets and Electronic Hierarchies', *Communications of the ACM* 30, 1987, pp. 484-497.

65 See, for example, Nohria Nitin, 'Is a Network Perspective a Useful Way of Studying Organizations?' in Nitin and Eccles, eds., *Networks and Organizations: Structure, Form, and Action*, Harvard Business School Press, Boston, 1992.

66 Malone and Yates 'Electronic Markets and Electronic Hierarchies', *Communications of the ACM* 30, 1987; see also, Thomas W. Malone, 'The Interdisciplinary Study of Coordination', *ACM Computing Surveys* 26, 1994, pp. 87-199.

67 Mark S. Granovetter, 'The Strength of Weak Ties', *American Journal of Sociology* 78, 1973, pp. 1360-80.

68 Max Weber, *Economy and Society*, University of California Press, Berkeley, 1978.

69 Kenneth J. Arrow, *The Limits of Organization*, W. W. Norton, New York, 1974.

70 This point is made in Masahiko Aoki, 'Toward an Economic Model of the Japanese Firm', *Journal of Economic Literature* 28, March 1990, pp. 1-27.

71 Ludwig von Mises, *Socialism. An Economic and Sociological Analysis*, Liberty Classics, Indianapolis, 1981; Friedrich A. Hayek, 'The Use of Knowledge in Society', *American Economic Review* 35, 1945, pp. 519-30.

72 See, for example, Kenneth J. Arrow, 'Classificatory Notes on the Production of Transmission of Technological Knowledge', *American Economic Review* 59, 1969, pp. 29-33.

73 Harry Katz,, *Shifting Gears: Changing Labor Relations in the US Automobile Industry*, MIT Press, Cambridge, 1985.

74 See James P. Womack and D. Jones, *The Machine that Changed the World: The Story of Lean Production*, Harper Perennial, New York, 1991.

75 Annalee Saxenian, *Regional Advantage: Culture and Competition in Silicon Valley and Route 128*, Harvard University Press, Cambridge, 1994.

76 In this respect, I wrongly overemphasized the importance of firm size in *Trust*. Large firm size can reflect social capital insofar as it involves the willingness of individuals to trust people outside of their immediate families; it can also reflect an absence of social capital, since it is possible to organize large firms on low trust, Taylorite lines. Firm size is much less important that the existence of social norms linking individuals. These norms can exist within the boundaries of a single organization; they can also transcend individual organizations.

77 Annalee Saxenian, *Regional Advantage: Culture and Competition in Silicon Valley and Route*

*128*, Harvard University Press, Cambridge, 1994, pp. 32-33.

78   Ibid. p. 33.

79   Masahiko Aoki, paper presented to the Samsung Economic Research Institute, June 1996.

80   See, for example, Edgar H. Schein, *Organizational Culture and Leadership*, Jossey-Bass, San Francisco, 1988.

81   Masahiko Aoki, 'The Japanese Firm as a System of Attributes: A Survey and Research Agenda', *Economie Industrielle*, 1994, pp. 83-108.

82   See Joseph B. White, 'Re-Engineering Gurus Take Steps to Remodel Their Stalling Vehicles', *Wall Street Journal*, November 26 1996, p. A1

## Part 3

83   Robert Axelrod, *The Evolution of Cooperation*, Basic Books, New York, 1984.

84   Strictly speaking, Coase himself did not postulate a 'Coase theorem'. Ronald H. Coase, 'The Problem of Social Cost', *Journal of Law and Economics* 3, 1960, pp. 1-44. This article is the single most commonly cited article in the legal literature today.

85   Andrew Sugden, 'Spontaneous Order', *Journal of Economic Perspectives* 3, 1989, pp. 85-97; Sugden, *The Economics of Rights, Co-operation and Welfare*, Blackwell, Oxford, 1986.

86   Robert C. Ellickson, *Order Without Law: How Neighbours Settle Disputes* Harvard University Press, Cambridge, 1991

87   On this point, see Jon Elster, 'Social Norms and Economic Theory', *Journal of Economic Perspectives* 3, 4, Fall 1989, pp. 99-117.

88   Field notes that for game theory to operate, the players have to agree to play by some set of pre-existing rules. Alexander James Field, 'Microeconomics, Norms, and Rationality' *Economic Development and Cultural Change* 32, July 1984, pp. 683-711

89   This is, of course, the broad point made by Dawkins in *The Selfish Gene*, Oxford University Press, New York, 1989.

90   Robert Trivers, 'The Evolution of Reciprocal Altruism', *Quarterly Review of Biology* 46, 1971, pp. 35-56.

91   I made a version of this argument in *Trust*, Free Press, New York, 1995.

92   Douglass C. North and, Robert P. Thomas, *The Rise of the Western World: A New Economic History*, Cambridge University Press, Cambridge, 1973.

93   Diego Gambetta, *The Sicilian Mafia: The business of private protection*, Harvard University Press, Cambridge, 1993.

94   Friedrich A. Hayek, *Law, Legislation, and Liberty*, University of Chicago Press, Chicago, 1983; *The Fatal Conceit*, University of Chicago Press, Chicago, 1988.

95   Ibid. p. 8.

96   There is by now a huge literature on this subject. For a layman's overview, see M. Mitchell Waldrop, *Complexity: The emerging science at the edge of order and chaos*, Simon and Schuster, New York, 1992 and Kevin Kelly, *Out of Control: The New Biology of Machines, Social Systems, and the Economic World*, Addison-Wesley, Reading, Mass. 1994. For more formal

accounts of spontaneous order, see John H. Holland, *Hidden Order: How Adaptation Builds Complexity*, Addison-Wesley, Reading, Mass, 1995;, Stuart A. Kauffman, *Origins of Order: Self-Organization and Selection in Evolution*, Oxford University Press, Oxford, 1992; and, Stuart A. Kauffman, *At Home in the Universe: The Search for the Laws of Self-Organization and Complexity*, Oxford University Press, New York and Oxford, 1995.

97  James S. Coleman, 'Social Capital in the Creation of Human Capital', *American Journal of Sociology Supplement* 94, 1988, S95-S120.

98  David Martin, *A General Theory of Secularization*, Harper and Row, New York, 1978; and Peter L. Berger, 'Secularism in Retreat', *National Interest* ,no. 46, 1996, pp. 3-12.

99  On American religiosity, see Seymour Martin Lipset, *American Exceptionalism: A Double-Edged Sword*, W.W. Norton, New York, 1995.

100  On this point, see Mark Granovetter, 'Problems of Explanation in Economic Sociology', in Nitin Nohria and Robert G. Eccles, eds., *Networks and Organizations: Structure, Form, and Action*, Harvard Business School Press, Boston, Mass., 1992, p. 38; see also Mary Ann Glendon's account of the 'lone rights bearer' in *Rights Talk: The Impoverishment of Political Discourse*, Free Press, New York, 1991, pp. 47-75.

101  Lionel Tiger, *Men in Groups*, Random House, New York, 1970.

102  James Q. Wilson, *The Moral Sense*, Free Press, New York, 1993.

103  See, for example, Edna Bonacich, 'A Theory of Middleman Minorities', *American Sociological Review* 38, 1972, pp. 583-594; Edna Bonacich and Jonathan H. Turner, 'Toward a Composite Theory of Middleman Minorities', *Ethnicity* 7, 1, pp. 144-158; Everett E. Hagen, *On the Theory of Social Change: How Economic Growth Begins*, Dorsey Press, Homewood, 1962; Alejandro Portes and Kenneth L. Wilson, 'Immigrant Enclaves: An Analysis of the Labor Market Experiences of Cubans in Miami', *American Journal of Sociology* 86, 1980, pp. 295-319; Ivan H. Light and Parminder Bhachu, eds., *Immigration and Entrepreneurship: Culture, Capital, and Ethnic Networks*, Transaction Publishers, New Brunswick, 1993; Ivan H. Light, 'Disadvantaged Minorities in Self-Employment', *International Journal of Comparative Sociology* 20, 1979, pp. 31-45.

104  Gary S. Becker, *A Treatise on the Family*, (enlarged edn.), Harvard University Press, Cambridge, 1991, p. 140.

105  David Popenoe, *Life Without Father: Compelling New Evidence that Fatherhood and Marriage are Indispensable for the Good of Children and Society*, Free Press, New York, 1996.

106  On the role of unit cohesion in the Second World War, see Martin van Creveld, *Fighting Power: German and US Army Performance, 1939-1945*, Greenwood Press, Westport, 1982.

107  For an overview of vocational and job-training programs, see Derek Bok, *The State of the Nation: Government and the Quest for a Better Society,* Harvard University Press, Cambridge, 1997.

108  For an overview, see Gertrude Himmelfarb, *The De-Moralization of Society: From Victorian Virtues to Modern Values*, Knopf, New York, 1995.

109  E. P. Thompson, *The Making of the English Working Class*, Penguin, London, 1963.

110  James Q. Wilson and Richard Herrnstein, *Crime and Human Nature*, Simon and Schuster, New York, 1985; Ted Robert Gurr and Hugh D. Graham, *Violence in America*, Signet, New

York, 1969; and Ted Robert Gurr, 'Contemporary Crime in Historical Perspective: A Comparative Study of London, Stockholm, and Sydney', *Annals* 434, 1977: pp. 114-136.

# Papers in Print

# Reports

# Occasional Papers

# Other Papers

Full Employment without Inflation
James Meade
£6.00

# Memoranda

1. Provider Choice: 'Opting In' through the Private Finance Initiative
Michael Fallon
£5.00

2. The Importance of Resource Accounting
Evan Davis
£3.50

3. Why There is No Time to Teach:
What is wrong with the National Curriculum 10 Level Scale
John Marks
£5.00

4. All Free Health Care Must be Effective
Brendan Devlin, Gwyn Bevan
£5.00

5. Recruiting to the Little Platoons
William Waldegrave
£5.00

6. Labour and the Public Services
John Willman
£8.00

7. Organising Cost Effective Access to Justice
Gwyn Bevan, Tony Holland and Michael Partington
£5.00

8. A Memo to Modernisers
Ron Beadle, Andrew Cooper, Evan Davis, Alex de Mont,
Stephen Pollard, David Sainsbury, John Willman
£8.00

9. Conservatives in Opposition: Republicans in the US
Daniel Finkelstein
£5.00

10. Housing Benefit: Incentives for Reform
Greg Clark
£8.00

11. The Market and Clause IV
Stephen Pollard
£5.00

12. Yeltsin's Choice: Background to the Chechnya Crisis
Vladimir Mau
£8.00

13. Teachers' Practices: A New Model for State Schools
Tony Meredith
£8.00

14 The Right to Earn: Learning to Live with Top People's Pay
Ron Beadle
£8.00

15. A Memo to Modernisers II
John Abbott, Peter Boone, Tom Chandos, Evan Davis, Alex de Mont, Ian Pearson MP,
Stephen Pollard, Katharine Raymond, John Spiers
£8.00

16. Schools, Selection and the Left
Stephen Pollard
£8.00

17. The Future of Long-Term Care
Andrew Cooper, Roderick Nye
£8.00

18. Better Job Options for Disabled People: Re-employ and Beyond
Peter Thurnham
£8.00

19. Negative Equity and the Housing Market
Andrew Cooper, Roderick Nye
£6.00

20. Industrial Injuries Compensation: Incentives to Change
Dr Greg Clark, Iain Smedley
£8.00

21. Better Government by Design: Improving the Effectiveness of Public Purchasing
Katharine Raymond, Marc Shaw
£8.00

22. A Memo to Modernisers III
    Evan Davis, John Kay, Alex de Mont, Stephen Pollard, Brian Pomeroy,
    Katharine Raymond
    £8.00

23. The Citizen's Charter Five Years On
    Roderick Nye
    £8.00

24. Standards of English and Maths in Primary Schools for 1995
    John Marks
    £10.00

25. Standards of Reading, Spelling and Maths for 7-year-olds in Primary Schools for 1995
    John Marks
    £10.00

26. An Expensive Lunch: The Political Economy of Britain's New Monetary Framework
    Robert Chote
    £10.00

# Trident Trust/SMF Contributions to Policy

1. Welfare to Work: The *America Works* Experience
   Roderick Nye (Introduction by John Spiers)
   £10.00

2. Job Insecurity vs Labour Market Flexibility
   David Smith (Introduction by John Spiers)
   £10.00

# Hard Data

1. The Rowntree Inquiry and 'Trickle Down'
   Andrew Cooper, Roderick Nye
   £5.00

2. Costing the Public Policy Agenda: A week of the *Today* Programme
   Andrew Cooper
   £5.00

3. Universal Nursery Education and Playgroups
   Andrew Cooper, Roderick Nye
   £5.00

4. Social Security Costs of the Social Chapter
   Andrew Cooper, Marc Shaw
   £5.00

5. What Price a Life?
   Andrew Cooper, Roderick Nye
   £5.00

# Centre for Post-Collectivist Studies

1. Russia's Stormy Path to Reform
   Robert Skidelsky (ed.)
   £20.00

2. Macroeconomic Stabilisation in Russia: Lessons of Reforms, 1992–1995
   Robert Skidelsky, Liam Halligan
   £10.00

3. The End of Order
   Francis Fukuyama
   £9.50

# Briefings

1. A Guide to Russia's Parliamentary Elections
   Liam Halligan, Boris Mozdoukhov
   £10.00